A STRAIGHTFORWA
BUSINESS

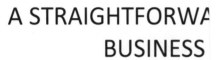

Robert Franks

Editor: Roger Sproston

Straightforward Publishing
www.straightforwardco.co.uk

Straightforward Guides

British Cataloguing in Publication data. A catalogue record is available for
this book from the British Library.

ISBN

978-1-84716-998-3

Printed in the United Kingdom by 4Edge www.4edge.co.uk

Cover Design by BW Studio Islington

CONTENTS

Introduction

****

Introduction

This Revised edition of a Straightforward Guide to Business Law is a wide ranging introduction to the law and practice as it affects and influences the environment that regulates business in the United Kingdom. The law is updated to December 2020.

Of course, as we all know we are in the throes of BREXIT and also the throes of a public health crisis. At the time of writing, the UK has left the EU and we are due to leave finally on December 31st 2020. In addition It may well be the case that certain areas of business law will be temporarily affected by the Corona virus, such as employment law and consumer law. This is because measures have had to be put into place to mitigate the effects of the virus.

EU law affects many areas of business and this book is written as we are at the end of the period of transition in December 2020. Where possible I have made reference to probable changes although there is a big unknown at the moment.

The book is intended for both the student and layperson and will also be suitable for the professional. Each chapter has relevant case law throughout which provides a suitable back drop to the subject matter.

The book begins with contract law, covering consideration and contracts, terms of contract, errors and contracts, contracts and illegality, duress and undue influence, discharge of a contract and remedies for breach of contract. Again, contract law, and the ability to seek remedies through the courts will have been affected. One of the main bones of contention will be that of *force majeure* or circumstances beyond control, and how COVID 19 has had an impact.

Negligence and duty of care is then discussed, covering causation, the liability of the employer and liability for dangerous products.

Remedies for negligence are also covered. Employment law is covered, covering a general outline of law plus discrimination and termination of employment. In addition, company law is covered in depth.

Finally, we discuss the all important area of intellectual property. Patents, trade marks, copyright, infringement of copyright plus design law are covered. This is one area that will be affected by BREXIT.

All of the main areas that relate to business law in the United Kingdom are covered in depth. The book should prove ideal to all of those who wish to enhance their knowledge of this important area.

****

Ch. 1

Business law-The Law of Contract

Underpinning all contracts are four main principles:

1) A contract is an agreement between the parties to that contract-one person makes an offer and the other accepts that offer

2) Both parties have an intention to be legally bound by the agreement-this is usually known as an intention to create legal relations

3) Parties to the agreement need to be absolutely clear as to the terms of the agreement – this is the main area of contention with contracts, as we will see later

4) There must be consideration provided by each of the parties to the contract – this means that one person promises to give or deliver and the other promises to pay. The offer and the payment – either monetary or in kind - is the consideration. When making a contract, or entering into a contract all parties to the contract must have the legal capacity to enter into a contract. Very importantly, a contract, in most cases, does not have to be in writing – a piece of paper is not necessary, the agreement and evidence of that agreement forms the basis of contract. There are a few important exceptions, including contracts relating to interests in land (Law of property (Miscellaneous Provisions) Act 1989, s 2(1) and consumer credit (Consumer Credit Act 1974). We will outline those contracts that do need to be in writing later on in this chapter. Other factors affecting formation include:

Form-the way the contract is created (e.g. the sale of land can only be made in the form of a deed). Form is an issue with specialty contracts but not with simple contracts

Privity of contract and the rights of third parties-generally a contract is only enforceable by or against a party to it, subject to exceptions and certain third party rights are now protected in the Contracts (Rights of Third Parties) Act 1999.

The nature of contracts – unilateral and bilateral contracts

The majority of contracts entered into are known as bilateral contracts. This quite simply means that each party to a contract agrees to take on an obligation. This obligation is underpinned by a promise to give something to the other party. A unilateral contract will arise where one party to the contract will make a promise to do something (usually to pay a sum of money) if the other party carries out a certain task. Examples of this are where you might undertake to pay someone a sum of money if they shave off their hair for charity or give up smoking. Estate agents enter into unilateral contracts whereby a percentage of sales go to the agent if they sell the property. However, the agent is not legally bound to sell the property, just to try to sell it.

The notion of offer and acceptance

As we have seen, for a contract to have legal status, usually one of the parties to the contract must have made an offer and the other party must have accepted the offer. Once the contract is accepted the agreement will be legally binding. The person making the offer is called the offeror and the person to whom the offer is made is known as the offeree. An offer may be express or implied. Express means that there is an express intention to offer goods and for X to pay an amount for the goods. Implied may mean, for example, when purchasing something from a store. The act of taking goods to a checkout means that there is an implied offer to buy those goods.

When dealing with contracts, or the formation of a contract most offers are made to specific parties. However, offers can also be made to a group of people or to the public at large. One such example is where a reward is offered for information following a crime. One famous case dealing with offers to the public at large is Carlill v Carbolic Smokeball (1893) the defendants in this case were the manufacturers of 'smokeballs' popular at the time, which they claimed could prevent flu. They published adverts to this effect stating that anyone using their smoke balls and not being cured of flu would receive £100.

One person buying their smokeballs was a Mrs Carlill. It did not work and she claimed the £100. The manufacturers argument was to claim that their advert did not constitute a contract, since it was impossible to contract with the whole wide world. They claimed that they were not legally bound to pay the money. The court, needless to say, rejected this argument, which held that the advert did contract with the world. Mrs Carlill accepted the offer and duly claimed the £100. A contract such as the one above is usually a unilateral contract.

The invitation to treat
Certain kinds of transactions between parties might involve a preliminary stage where one party to the contract invites the other party to make an offer. This preliminary stage is known as 'invitation to treat'.

One such case that demonstrates this is that of Gibson v Manchester City Council (1979). In this case, a council tenant of Manchester City Council expressed an interest in buying their house. The application was duly completed and sent to the council. A letter was received from the council stating that it may be prepared to sell the house to the tenant for £2180. The tenant, Mr Gibson, queried the purchase price pointing out that the path to the house was in bad condition. The council refused to alter the price, stating that the valuation reflected the condition of the property and the current property market. Mr Gibson then wrote asking the council to continue with the sale. Following a change in the control of the council, and a new political approach, it was decided to stop the sale of houses to tenants. Mr Gibson was informed that his application had been declined, notwithstanding the initial offer. Legal proceedings were brought against the council claiming that the letter received by Mr Gibson, with the offer of sale at a price, constituted a contract, and was an offer which he duly accepted. The House of Lords, however, ruled that the council had not made an offer, the letter stating the purchase price was merely one step in the negotiations for a contract and amounted only to an invitation to treat. Its purpose in the first instance was quite simply to invite the making of a formal application, amounting to an offer, from the tenant.

Retailers websites

These are probably invitations to treat, although this has no clear definition at the moment. Regulation 12 of the E-Commerce (EC Directives) Regulations 2002 suggests that the customers order may well be the offer so that the website is an invitation to treat.

Offers of sale in shops

Goods in shop windows marked with a price are generally regarded as invitations to treat, rather than offers to actually sell the goods at the price displayed. One such case highlighting this is Fisher v Bell (1961) where a shopkeeper was prosecuted under the Offensive Weapons Act

1959 for 'offering for sale' an offensive weapon. The shopkeeper was displaying a flick knife with a price attached in the window. It was held that the display of the flick knife was an invitation to treat, rather than an offer, thus the shopkeeper was found not guilty of the offence.

Where goods are sold on a self-service basis, the customer will make an offer to purchase on presenting the goods at the till and the shopkeeper may reject or accept that offer. One case which highlights this is Pharmaceutical Society of Great Britain v Boots Cash Chemists (Southern) Limited 1953. Boots were charged with an offence concerning the sale of items, medicines that could only be sold under the supervision of a qualified pharmacist. Two customers in a self-service shop selected the items, which were marked with a price from a shelf in the shop. The shelves were not supervised by a pharmacist but the pharmacist was instructed to supervise at the cash desk. The issue was whether the sale had taken place at the shelf or the cash desk. The Court of Appeal decided that the shelf display was like an advertisement and was therefore an invitation to treat. The offer was made by the customer when the items were placed in a basket and was only accepted when the goods were taken to the cash desk. A pharmacist was supervising at that point so no offence was committed.

Following on from this principle, shops do not have to sell goods at the marked price and a customer cannot insist on buying a particular good on display. Displaying the goods is not an offer so a customer cannot accept it making a binding contract. (In reality, if shops do display goods at a price they generally sell it at that price although, as we have seen they do not have to).

Contracts and advertisements

A distinction is generally made between advertisements for unilateral contracts and advertisements for bilateral contracts. Advertisements

11

for unilateral contracts will include those such as described in the case of Carlill and Carbolic Smokeball Co or those offering a reward for information or for lost property. They are usually treated as offers on the basis that no further negotiations are needed between the parties to the offer and the person making the offer will usually be bound by it. One case is that of Bowerman v Association of British Travel Agents Ltd (1996) in which a school had booked a skiing holiday with a travel agent, which was a member of ABTA. Any member of ABTA has to display a notice as follows:

Where holidays or other travel arrangements have not yet commenced at the time of failure of the tour operator, ABTA arranges for you to be reimbursed the money you have paid for your holiday.

In this case the tour operator became insolvent and all holidays were cancelled. The school was refunded the money paid for the holiday but not the cost of the travel insurance taken out, which was significant. The case was taken to court and ABTA lost because the notice constituted an offer which the school accepted by contracting with the ABTA member.

Bilateral contracts

Bilateral contracts are the types that advertise specified goods at a certain price such as those found in shop windows and in magazines. They are usually considered invitations to treat on the grounds that they may lead to further bargaining. One such case that highlights this is Partridge v Crittendon (1968). An advertisement in a magazine stated 'Bramblefinch cocks and hens 25shillings each'. As the Bramblefinch was a protected species, the person who placed the advert was charged with unlawfully offering for sale a wild bird which was against the Protection of Birds Act 1954, but the conviction was quashed on the grounds that the advertisement was not an offer but an invitation to treat.

Communication of offers

A valid offer must be communicated to the offeree. It would be unfair for a person to be bound by an offer of which he had no knowledge. This is reflected in Taylor v Laird 1856. The offeree must have clear knowledge of the existence of an offer for it to be enforceable. This is reflected in Inland Revenue Commissioners v Fry 2001.

An offer can be made to one individual or to the whole world, when the offer can be accepted by any party who had genuine notice of it. In addition, the terms of the contract must be certain. The parties must know in advance what they are contracting over, so any vague words may invalidate the agreement. this is reflected in Guthing v Lynn 1831.

The length of time an offer should last

An offer may cease to exist in any of the following circumstances:

-Where an offeror states that an offer will be open for a specified time

-Where the offeror has not specified how long the offer will remain open, the offer will lapse after a reasonable length of time has passed. How much time can be deemed reasonable will depend on whether the offer was communicated quickly and also on the subject matter.

Some offers are made subject to certain specified conditions, and if these conditions are not in place, the offer may lapse. An offer may lapse if and when the offeree rejects it. For example, if A offers to sell B a car on Tuesday, and B says no, B cannot come back on Wednesday and insist on accepting the offer

A counter offer can terminate the original offer. One case that highlights this is Hyde v Wrench (1840) where the defendant offered to sell his farm for £1000 and the plaintiff responded by offering to buy it at £950-this is termed making a counter offer. The farm owner refused to sell at that price and when the plaintiff later tried to buy the farm at £1000, the original asking price, it was held that this offer was no longer available. The counter offer had terminated the original offer

The death of the offeror can affect the offer. If the offeree knows of the death of the offeror then the offer is terminated. If they did not, the offer still stands, although this is one area of law that is still unclear. It very much depends on the circumstances at the time

An offer may be revoked, withdrawn, at any time until it has been accepted. This is the basic rule, although there are a number of other principles. It is not enough for an offeror simply to change his or her mind about an offer. The offeror must notify the offeree that the offer has been revoked. Revocation does not specifically have to be communicated by the offeror, it can be by another reliable party.

Acceptance of an offer
For acceptance to be valid the following conditions must be met:
- Acceptance must be communicated to the seller: the buyer must receive the acceptance to be effective (*Entorres v Miles Far East* (1955)); silence will not suffice (*Felthouse v Bindley* (1862)); acceptance can be made through conduct (*Butler Machine Tool v Ex-cell-o Corporation* (1979)).
- The terms of the acceptance must exactly match the terms of the offer: if the terms are not the same, this will actually be a counter offer and no contract will have arisen (*Hyde v Wrench* (1840)).

The agreement must be certain (see below).

Consideration is something of legal value which is given in exchange for something else. It can be anything of value (eg, money, property, or a service), which each party to a legally binding contract must agree to exchange if the contract is to be valid. In *Currie v Misa* (1875), Lush J referred to consideration as consisting of a detriment to the promisee or a benefit to the promisor. He described it as: '...some right, interest, profit or benefit accruing to one party, or some forebearance, detriment, loss or responsibility given, suffered or undertaken by the other.'

Certainty of agreement

Even though the parties may have appeared to make an agreement by the exchange of a matching offer and acceptance, the courts may refuse to enforce it if there appears to be uncertainty about what has been agreed, or if some important aspect of the agreement is left open to be decided later.

In *Scammell v Ouston* (1941), for example, the parties had agreed to the supply of a lorry on 'hire purchase terms'. The House of Lords held that in the absence of any other evidence of the details of the hire purchase agreement this was too vague to be enforceable, and there was therefore no contract.

Acceptance of an offer must be unconditional, accepting the precise terms of the offer. Where the process of negotiation is long and difficult, it might be difficult to pinpoint exactly when an offer has been made and accepted. In such cases a court will examine the precise course of negotiations to ascertain whether the parties have reached agreement, if at all and when. This process can be complicated when the so-called 'battle of forms' occurs. Rather than negotiating terms each time a contract is made many companies try to use standard conditions, which will be printed on headed stationary, such as order forms and delivery notes. The 'battle of forms' occurs when one party sends a form stating that the contract is on their terms, and the other party responds by sending back the forms and stating that the contract is on their terms. The general rule in these cases is that the 'last shot' wins the battle. Each new form issued is treated as a counter offer, so that when one party performs its obligation under the contract the action will be seen as acceptance by the other side. One simple case that illustrates this is British Road Services v Crutchley (Arthur V) Ltd (1968). The plaintiffs delivered some whisky to the defendants for storage. The BRS driver handed the defendants a delivery note, which listed the company's terms of carriage. The note was accepted and stamped with Crutchley's terms and conditions and the court held that by accepting this, the BRS driver had accepted a counter offer. Although many cases are simple, other more recent case law has held that the last shot will not always succeed.

It is a basic assumption that there is no acceptance until the act has been thoroughly performed. However, in some cases, part performance may amount to acceptance. In Errington v Errington (1952) a father bought a house in his own name for £750, borrowing £500 of the price from a building society. He bought the house for his son and daughter in law to live in, and told them that they must meet the mortgage repayments. If they met the payments the house would be signed over to them on completion of the term. The couple moved in and began to pay the mortgage, but they never in fact made the promise to continue with the payments until the mortgage was paid off, which meant that the contract was unilateral.

When the father later died, the people in charge of his affairs sought to withdraw the offer. The Court of Appeal held that it was too late to do this. The part performance of the son and daughter in law constituted an acceptance of the contract and the father and his representatives after death were bound by the resulting contract unless the son and daughter in law ceased the payments, in which case the offer was no longer binding.

A request for information about an offer does not constitute a counter offer, so the original offer remains open. If an offeree has to accept an offer in a specified manner, then only acceptance by that method or an equally effective one will be binding

Communicating acceptance of an offer

An acceptance will not usually take effect until it is clearly communicated to the offeror. However, there are some circumstances where acceptance may take effect without it being communicated to the offeror. An offer may clearly state, or indeed imply, that acceptance need not be communicated to the offeror. An offeror who fails to receive an acceptance through their own fault may be prevented from claiming that the non-communication means they should not be bound by the contract.

The general rule for acceptances by post is that they take effect when they are posted, rather than when they are communicated. The postal rule was laid down in the case of Adams v Lindsell (1818), when on the 2nd of September 1817, the defendants wrote to the plaintiffs, who were in the wool processing business, offering to sell them a quantity of sheep fleeces, and stating that they required an answer 'in course of post'. However, the defendants did not address the letter correctly and it did not reach the plaintiffs until the evening of September the 5th. The plaintiffs posted their acceptance the same evening, and it reached the defendants on the 9th of September. If the original letter had been correctly addressed it would have reached the plaintiffs by the 7th of September. Because it was incorrectly addressed it did not and no reply was received and the wool was sold to a third party. The issue was whether a sale had been made before the sale of the wool to the third party. The court heard that the contract was concluded as soon as the acceptance was posted and that the defendants were bound from the evening of 5th September so should not have sold the wool to a third party. There are certain exceptions to the postal rule. The offeror may avoid the postal rule by making it a specific term of their offer that acceptance will only take effect when it is communicated to them.

The postal rule has limited application to modern communications technology. In Entores Ltd v Miles Far East Corp, offer and acceptance communicated by telex were valid because the method was so instantaneous that the parties were deemed to be dealing as if face-to-face, even though they were in different countries. The time when these forms of communication are used may cause problems in determining if a contract is made, as when a fax is sent out of office hours.

Now offer and acceptance in the case of electronic communication is governed by the Consumer Contracts (Information, Cancellation and Additional Charges) Regulations 2013 which replaced the Consumer Protection (Distance Selling) Regulations 2000. This gives the buyer the right to be informed of the right to cancel within seven days, description, price, arrangements for payment and identity of seller, and to be given written confirmation, without which a contract is not formed. Under EU Electronic Commerce Directive 2000/31 no contract can be made electronically until the buyer has received acknowledgement of his acceptance. the Directive has been implemented through the Electronic Commerce (EC Directive) Regulations 2000.

Ignorance of the offer

It is generally accepted that a person cannot accept an offer of which they are unaware, because in order to create a binding contract, the parties must reach agreement. This is a very important principle.

Tenders, auctions and the sale of land

The rules outlined above also apply to the sale of land and to sales by tender and auction. If a large organization, such as a company or government department needs to contract a supplier of goods or services, it will, more often than not, advertise for tenders, i.e., bids. Organizations wishing to supply goods or services will reply, detailing price for these services. The advertiser will choose from the replies and contact the successful tender. As a general rule, the request for tenders is regarded as an invitation to treat, (see previous) so there is no specific obligation to accept any of the tenders sent. The tenders themselves are offers and a contract does not come into existence until one is accepted. However, where a party has issued an invitation to tender, it is bound to consider all correctly submitted tenders. One such case highlighting this is Blackpool and Fylde Aero Club v Blackpool Borough Council (1990). Blackpool BC invited tenders from people who were interested in operating leisure flights from the local airfield. Tenders had to be submitted to the town hall by a stated deadline. The Aero Club submitted its application on time but the council refused to consider it, as due to an error on their part, they mistakenly believed that the tender had been submitted after the deadline.

It was held that the council's invitation to tender was a unilateral offer to consider all tenders which fell within its rules. The tender constituted an offer which had been accepted by the Aero Club. The offer was accepted by any party who put in a tender. Thus the council were obliged to consider all tenders (acceptances) to their offer,

19

including the Aero Club tender. They were not, of course, obliged to accept the tender. In some cases however, an invitation for tenders may in itself be an offer. The main example of this is where the invitation to tender makes it clear that the lowest tender (or highest) will be accepted. The implications of choosing to accept a tender depend on what sort of tender is involved.

Specific tenders

Where an invitation to tender specifies that a particular quantity of goods is required on a particular date, or between certain dates, agreeing to one of the tenders submitted will constitute acceptance of an offer, creating a contract between the parties.

Non-specific tenders

Some invitations to tender are not specific, and may for example simply state that certain goods may be required, up to a particular maximum quantity, with deliveries to be made if and when requested. For example, an invitation to tender made by a hospital may ask for tenders to supply goods, if and when required. In this case, taking up one of the tenders submitted does not amount to acceptance of an offer in the contractual sense and there is no contract. The hospital may take the goods all at once, some at a time or none at all. It is not bound.

Auction sales

The parties to an auction sale are the bidder and the owner of the goods. The auctioneer supplies a service and is not party to the contract between buyer and seller.

Sale of land

The standard rules of contract apply to the sale of land, including buildings. However, the court applies the rules strictly in the case of land, tending to require very clear evidence of an intention to be bound before they will state that an offer has been made.

In Harvey v Facey (1893) the plaintiffs sent the defendants a telegram asking 'will you sell us Bumper Hall Pen? Telegraph lowest cash price'. The reply arrived back stating 'Lowest price for Bumper Hall pen £900'. The plaintiffs then sent a telegram saying 'we agree to buy Bumper Hall Pen for £900. Please send us your title deeds'. On these facts, the Privy Council held that there was no contract. They regarded the telegram from the defendants as a statement of price only. It was therefore not an offer which could be accepted by the third telegram.

In practice there are rigid procedures involved in the sale of land. The first is the 'sale subject to contract', where the parties agree to the sale and the implication is that there is a good deal of proving and other work before a contract is in existence. The next stage is the exchange of contract, where the buyer and seller agree to the terms of the formal contract. Once the contracts are exchanged then the contract is binding and any backing out can result in a claim for damages and lost deposit.

Certainty of contract

In order to be viewed as a binding contract, an agreement must be absolutely certain. That is, it should not be vague or incomplete. One such case that amplifies this is that of Scammell v Ouston (1941) where the parties agreed that Ouston could buy a van from Scammell, giving his lorry in part exchange paying the balance over two-years on hire purchase terms. Scammell decided to back out and claimed that there was no contract between the parties. The House of Lords agreed, pointing out that the courts would uphold an agreement if there really was one, in this case the terms were too vague, particularly the agreement to pay on Hire Purchase Terms. In certain cases, parties may leave details vague, particularly when dealing with fluctuating prices and other factors. Provisions should be in the contract stating how they should be clarified.

Terms implied into contract by statute

In some cases, statute will override contract and will provide that certain provisions should be read into contracts even though they have not been specifically agreed between the parties. For example, under the Consumer Rights Act 2015, an agreement for the sale of goods can become binding as soon as the parties have agreed to buy and sell, with the details of the contract being laid down by law, or determined by the standard of reasonableness. In such a case, the parties do not even have had to agree on a price. The buyer is entitled to pay a reasonable price. Terms implied by statute will be examined further on in this book.

Intention to create legal relations

One major principle of contract law is that of intention to create legal relations. If two or more parties make an agreement without the intention of being legally bound by it, the agreement will not be regarded as a contract. As far as intent to be legally bound is concerned, contracts can be divided into domestic and social agreements on one hand, and commercial agreements on the other. Where the agreement falls into the former category there is an assumption that the parties do not intend to create legal relations. The reverse is true when it comes to commercial agreements.

Domestic and social agreements

Where a husband and wife who are living together as one household make an agreement, the courts will assume that they do not intend to be legally bound, unless the agreement states other wise. In Balfour v Balfour (1919) the defendant was a civil servant stationed in Sri Lanka. Whilst the couple were on leave in England, Mrs. Balfour was taken ill, and it became clear that her husband would have to return by himself. He promised to pay her maintenance of £30 per month. They eventually separated and the husband refused to make any more payments. The Court of Appeal decided he was not bound to make further payments, as when the agreement was made there was no intention to create legal relations. Likewise, agreements between parents and children are assumed not to be legally binding.

Social agreements

The presumption that an agreement is not intended to be legally binding is also applied to social relationships between people who are not related. With both the above though, there can be exceptions.
Commercial agreements

There is a strong presumption in commercial agreements that the parties intend to be legally bound, and unless clear words are used this presumption stands. Where the words of a business agreement are ambiguous, the courts will favor the interpretation that suggests that the parties did intend to create legal relations.

The capacity to enter into a contract

The law states that individuals who enter into a contract must have the capacity to enter into a contract, otherwise it is voidable. Adults who have full capacity are able to enter into contracts and enforce them at law (unless they are illegal contracts).

The law sets out those who do not have legal capacity to contract, particularly providing special legal protection to those who are minors, or under a mental disability.

Minors and capacity in contract law

Individuals who are under the age of 18 are known as 'minors' under the Family Reform Act 1969. A minor can enter into a contract at law, however, such a contract is 'voidable' by the minor before they reach 18 (and for a time thereafter). This means that the minor can enforce the contract, but they can also terminate it if they wish. Once the minor reaches the age of 18, the contract becomes legally binding on both parties. However, there are exceptions to the general rule: a minor may need to enter into a contract to buy necessities, such as food, clothing, medicine and other things necessary for them and their lifestyle. Minors may also need to enter into legally binding contracts for their education, such as apprenticeships.

These types of contract are enforceable against the minor, however, such contracts must be fair to be enforceable against the minor. So if a minor pays a reasonable price for items required in the circumstances, the minor is legally required to fulfil the contract (i.e. pay for the goods or service).

A case where such a contract has been enforced is that of *Doyle v White City Stadium* (1935), where there was an agreement to train a boxer. There was no money paid, but the contract was enforceable as it was considered that the contract was beneficial because of the training provided. Another case where the contract was held enforceable is *Clements v London & NW Rail Co* (1894) where certain benefits were removed following a contract of employment, but the contract was considered to be beneficial and was upheld.

When can a contract with minors be voided?

The courts may not uphold a contract if it is considered not to be to the benefit of the minor. For example, in the case of *De Francesco v Barnum* (1889), a minor aged 14 years old, entered into an agreement to train as a dancer on stage. However, the contract had conditions which were considered not beneficial to the minor and, therefore, the minor was not bound by the contact. More recently, in the 2006 case of *Proform Sports Management Ltd v Proactive Sports Management Ltd* the court had to consider a contract entered into by footballer Wayne Rooney (who was 17 at the time) with his agent. The High Court ruled that the contract was voidable because it was not an agreement equivalent to contracts of apprenticeship, education and service.

A 'voidable contract' is a contract that can be ended. The contract is still valid, but it can be avoided by the minor who can legally terminate the agreement – before reaching the age of 18 years, or within a reasonable time of coming of age. What is a reasonable time period will depend on the facts of the case.

In the case of *Steinberg v Scala (Leeds) Ltd* (1923), the contract was voided because the minor was unable to keep up with payments. However, in the case of *Edwards v Carter* (1892) the court decided that the contract could not be rejected and the agreement was enforceable.

What happens if money has already been paid by a minor?

If money is paid by a minor under a contract, then usually this cannot be recovered unless it can be proved that the contract has not been beneficial to the minor. So if a minor enjoys goods or services, then seeks to terminate the contract and recover money already paid – he cannot be reimbursed.

In the case of *Pearce v Brain* (1929), a minor exchanged a motor cycle for a car, but found that the car had defects. The court decided that the contract must stand as he had used the car and, therefore, had enjoyed the benefit of it.

The Minors' Contracts Act 1987

This Act was introduced to protect minors alongside the common law (i.e. rulings of the courts). This Act also provides guarantees for minors contracting with adults. A contract is binding on the adult but not on the minor; however, if the minor ratifies the contract after having reaching the age of 18 by, for instance, an act confirming a promise made when a minor – he is legally bound. Furthermore, the contact is not void while still a minor – and any money paid under the contract terms cannot be repaid unless there has been no benefit received.

However, there are exceptions, the most likely of which to arise is that of a contract for 'necessities' as discussed above.

Corporations

A corporation is a legal entity that is treated by law as having a separate identity from the persons who constitute it. There are three main types of corporation: registered companies, corporations established by statute and chartered corporations. Each has a different level of contracting ability.

Registered companies

These are companies registered under the Companies Act 2006, which superseded the 1985 Companies Act and which covers most commercial companies. When registering, companies must supply a document that regulates their activities called a memorandum of association, which contains information including an objects clause, laying down the range of activities that their company can engage in. Under the 1989 Companies Act, which has been replaced by the 2006

Act a company can be liable for a contract made outside its stated activities if the other party has acted in good faith.

Statutory companies

These corporations are created by an Act of Parliament, for specific purposes, the Independent Broadcasting Authority is an example, as are local authorities. The statute creating the particular corporation will specify the purposes for which that corporation may make contracts. Any contracted outside of these purposes is null and void.

Chartered corporations

These are corporations set up by Royal Charter, which means that their rights are officially granted by the Crown. Examples are charities and some universities and other educational institutions. They have the same contractual capacity as an adult human being.

Formalities

We have discussed the fact that an agreement, with some exceptions, does not have to take a specific written form in order to be deemed a binding contract.

A contract can be oral. One famous recent case involving an oral contract was Hadley v Kemp (1990) where Gary Kemp was the songwriter in the group Spandau Ballet. He was sued by other members of the group for royalties received for the group's music. The basis of the claim was that there was an oral agreement to share royalties.

They were unable to prove the existence of any oral agreement and their claim failed.

*

Contracts which must be made by deed

The Law of Property Act 1925 states that a contract for a lease of more than three years must be made by deed, which basically means that it must be put into a formal document, signed in front of witnesses.

Contracts which must be in writing

Some statutes lay down that certain types of contract must be in writing. Most contracts involving sales of land must be in writing, under the Law of Property Act 1989. Other contracts that need to be in writing are those involving the transfers of shares in a limited company (Companies Act 2006 , bills of exchange; cheques and promissory notes (Bills of Exchange Act (1882); and regulated consumer credit agreements, such as hire purchase agreements (Consumer Credit Act 1974, as amended by the 2006 Consumer Credit Act).

Contracts which must be evidenced in writing

Contracts of guarantee (where one party guarantees the obligations of another, such as parents guaranteeing a sons or daughters overdraft) are required to be 'evidenced in writing'. Contracts for sale or disposition of land before 27th September 1989 are still covered by the old law prior to the Law of Property Act 1989. Evidenced in writing means that although the contract itself may not be a written one, there must be written evidence of the transaction. The evidence must have existed before one party tried to enforce the contract against the other, and it must be signed by the party against whom the contract is to be enforced.

Electronic contracts

Many transactions and other forms of trade are now conducted electronically. For example, most people will at least be familiar with, if not frequent users of, ATMs situated outside or inside banks. When a bank's customer withdraws money or uses an ATM for other purposes, an electronic transaction takes place. More and more business is now done electronically, often with the parties never physically meeting each other. Online shops, for example, allow potential customers to browse, select and purchase goods without ever asking a salesperson for advice or assistance. Negotiations, giving quotes or submitting tenders for work may all be done electronically and indeed are. A great deal of information is now passed electronically within organisations and from one organisation to another. This all raises a number of legal questions, specifically with regard to electronic contracts. Some of the most important issues include whether an electronic contract is valid, that is, whether it must comply with certain formalities, whether electronic signatures are admissible as evidence of intent and agreement, and what law applies to an electronic contract (if it is between international parties). These issues are addressed overleaf.

Formalities of an electronic contract

Generally, as we have seen, contracts can take any number of forms. They can be by deed, in writing, evidenced in writing, oral, or implied from the conduct of the parties. Certain contracts, however, require a specific form, and will not be legal (though they may be equitable) if they fail to comply with the formalities. For example, as we have seen, a conveyance of land or any interest in land must, under s52 of the Law of Property Act 1925, be by deed, save for the exceptions listed in that section. Other contracts are required to be in writing. So what form, if any, must an electronic contract take? The answer depends on the nature of the contract. If writing is a requirement, do documents which are stored digitally on a computer hard drive comply? Schedule

1 to the Interpretation Act 1978 states: "'Writing' includes typing, printing, lithography, photography and other modes of representing or reproducing words in a visible form, and expressions referring to writing are construed accordingly." Since words stored digitally on a computer may be reproduced on a monitor or printed onto paper, it would appear that computer storage is covered by this definition. Nevertheless, individual cases may still have to be decided by the courts.

Electronic signatures

A signature is generally understood as evidence that the signatory approves of a document's contents. But does this ring true also for a person's name printed on a telex or fax, or reproduced in electronic mail? In Good Challenger Navegante SA v Metalexportimport SA (2004) the Court of Appeal held that for the purposes of s30 of the Limitation Act 1980 a typed name on a telex was a signature. The Court held that "...the typed name of the sender at the end of the telex not only identified the maker but led to the inference that he had approved the contents." This does not apply to all instances of typed names, however, and a formal contract with typed names at the end with spaces underneath where the parties are expected to write their names would be unlikely to fall within the reasoning given in the Good Challenger case.

Above all, the signature must be able to objectively show that the signatory, by signing or printing their name, approved of a document's contents and intended to be bound by them. It is irrelevant whether the contents have been read (unless there has been some misrepresentation). The courts confirmed in Mehta v J Pereira Fernandes SA (2006) that a person's name which is shown as part of an email address in the header of an email does not mean that the person intended to be legally bound by the contents of the email. The automatic insertion of an email address could not be considered as a signature. Under s7 of the Electronic Communications Act 2000 an electronic signature is anything in electronic form which:

- is incorporated into or otherwise logically associated with any electronic communication or electronic data, and
- is certified as such by the signatory

Such a signature is admissible in evidence for the purpose of establishing the authenticity, the integrity, or both, of the electronic communication or data.

Certification of the signature requires the signatory to make a statement that the signature, its production, communication or verification, or a procedure applied to it, is a valid means of establishing the authenticity, integrity or both of the electronic communication or data.

Contracts concluded electronically

Article 9 of Directive 2000/31/EC, on electronic commerce, requires EU member states to ensure both that contracts can be concluded by electronic means and that the law does not create any barriers against using such contracts or which deprive such contracts of their validity. In the UK, the Electronic Communications Act 2000 supports approved cryptography service providers and provides that electronic signatures are admissible in evidence. Some contracts, though, such as those which transfer rights in real estate, are exempt from these general principles. Article 10 of Directive 2000/31/EC requires certain information to be provided regarding electronic contracts, such as describing the technical steps to be followed to conclude the contract, and the technical means for identifying and correct input errors before placing orders.

****

1.2

Consideration and Contracts

As we saw in chapter 2, English law states that a contract is not usually binding unless it is supported by consideration. Consideration is usually said to mean that each party to a contract must give something in return for what is gained from the other party. Very basically, if there is a dispute and you wish to enforce someone's promise to you, then you must prove that you gave something in return for that promise. The key case that defined 'consideration' is *Currie v Misa* (1875), which states that consideration can consist of a right, interest, profit, benefit, detriment or forbearance. There are two types of consideration: executed and executory, as described below.

Consideration may be goods or services, a thing or a service. Many problems concerning consideration arise not when a contract is made but when one or other of the parties to the contract seeks to modify it, such as paying a lower price than agreed or supplying a different good or service.

Promisor and Promisee
In most contracts, it is the case that two promises will be exchanged, so each party to the contract is promisor and promisee. In a contract case, the claimant will often be arguing that the defendant has broken the promise made to the claimant and therefore the claimant will usually be the promisee. One example is if A contracts to build a conservatory and B promises to pay £5000 for the conservatory, there are two promises in this contract. A's promise to build a conservatory

and B's promise to pay. If A fails to build the conservatory B can sue him. If the issue of consideration arises, B will seek to prove that his promise to pay £5000 was consideration for A's promise for building the conservatory. In that action, A will be the promisor and B the promisee. However, reverse the situation and B fails to pay, then A will sue and, if consideration is at issue, A will have to prove that his promise to build the conservatory was consideration for B's promise to pay. In that action, A will be the promisee and B the promisor.

'Executory' and 'executed' consideration

As mentioned above, consideration can fall into two categories: executory and executed. Executed consideration is the performance of an act in return for a promise. Executory consideration is when the person makes a promise, and the other person offers a counter promise – you promise to deliver goods to me and I promise to pay for them when they arrive, the promise is executory because it is something to be done in the future.

Consideration must be given in return for the promise or act of the other party. Something done, given, or promised beforehand will not be counted as consideration. A classic case concerning this arose in Roscorla v Thomas (1842). The defendant sold the plaintiff a horse. After the sale was completed, the defendant told the plaintiff that the animal was 'sound and free from any vice'. This was not the actual truth and the plaintiff sued. The court held that the defendants promise was unenforceable, because it was made after the sale. If the promise about the horse's condition had been made before, the plaintiff would have provided consideration for it by buying the horse. As it was made after the sale, the consideration was past, for it had not been given in return for the promise.

There are two exceptions to the rule that past consideration is no consideration. The first is where the past consideration was provided at the promisors request, and it was understood that payment would be made. The second is the bill of exchange. Under s27 of the Bills of Exchange Act 1882, an antecedent debt or 'liability' may be consideration for receipt of a bill of exchange.

The rules of consideration
Consideration need not be adequate
The law of contract regulates the making of bargains. As freedom of contract is vital, the law is not concerned with whether a party has made a good bargain or a bad one. Adequacy is given its normal meaning-the contract is enforceable even if the price does not match the value of what is being gained under the agreement. One such case that reflects this is Thomas v Thomas (1842). Before he died Thomas expressed a wish that his wife should be allowed to remain in his house although there was no mention of this in his will. The executors carried out his wish but charged the widow a nominal ground rent of £1 a year. When they later tried to dispossess her they failed.

Consideration must be sufficient
Consideration offered is sufficient provided that:
It is real (White v Bluett (1853)
It is tangible (Ward v Byham (1956)
It has some discernible value (Chappel v Nestle (1960); and
Economic value is measured against benefit gained.

Consideration must not be past
Consideration must follow rather than precede agreement. This prevents coercion by suppliers of goods and services.

Consideration must be of economic value

What this principle basically means is that there must be some physical value, rather than just an emotional or sentimental value.

Consideration can be a promise not to sue

If one party has a possible civil claim against the other, a promise not to enforce that claim is good consideration for a promise given in return. One clear example is if A crashes into B's car then A can promise not to sue if B pays for the damage.

Performance of an existing duty

Where a promisee already owes the promisor a legal duty, then in theory performing that duty should not in itself be consideration. If the promisee does nothing more than they are already obliged to do, they are suffering no detriment and the promisor is only getting a benefit to which he or she is entitled.

Existing duties can be divided into three categories: public duties; contractual duties to the promisor; and contractual duties to a third party.

Existing public duty

Where a person is merely carrying out duties they are legally bound to perform – such as police officer or juror, doing that alone will not be consideration. However, where a promisee is under a public duty, but does something beyond the call of that duty, that extra act amounts to consideration. In Glasbrook Brothers v Glamorgan County Council (1925) the owners of a South Wales Mine asked the police to place a guard at their colliery during a strike. The police suggested that regular checks by mobile patrol would be adequate but the owners replied that they wanted something more intensive and the police agreed at an extra cost of £2,200. After the strike the owners refused to pay saying that the police had a duty to protect their property. The courts held in favor of the police saying that the police did not have a duty to supply the cover they did, only the cover they deemed sufficient. Anything over and above was deemed consideration.

Existing contractual duty to the promisor

The position on contractual duties and consideration has changed from the traditional position whereby the performance of an existing contractual duty owed to a promisor was not consideration. In Stilk v Myrick (1809) two sailors deserted a ship during a voyage and the captain was unable to find replacements. The remaining crew-members were promised extra wages for sailing the ship back to London but the captain refused to pay on arrival and the sailors sued with the court holding that there was no consideration as the sailors had already contracted to sail the boat back to its destination. In Hartley v Ponsonby (1857) half the crew deserted and the remaining crew were offered extra wages to carry on the journey. At the end the captain refused to pay and the crew sued and won, as the courts held that there was consideration as the crew were to small to sail the boat adequately and extra money was justified.

An exception to the rule that performance of an existing contractual obligation owed to the promisor will not amount to consideration will occur where a party can be seen to receive an extra benefit from the other party's agreement to carry out his existing obligations. One such case that highlights this is that of Williams v Roffey Brothers (1991). In this case the defendants (the main contractors) were refurbishing a block of flats. They sub-contracted the carpentry works to the plaintiff. The plaintiff ran into financial difficulties, whereupon the defendants agreed to pay the plaintiff an additional sum if they completed the work on time. It was held that where a party to an existing contract later agrees to pay an 'extra bonus' in order that the other party performs his obligations under the original contract, then the new agreement is binding if the party agreeing to pay the bonus has thereby obtained some new practical advantage or avoided a disadvantage. In this particular case, the advantage was the avoidance of a penalty clause and the expense of finding new carpenters, among other factors.

Existing contractual duty to a third party

In some cases two parties make a contract to provide a benefit to a third party. If one of the parties (A) makes a further promise to that third party to provide the benefit they have already contracted to provide, that further promise can be good consideration for a promise made by the third party in return-even though nothing more than the contractual duty is being promised by A.

One case that illustrates this is Scotson v Pegg (1861).

Scotson contracted to supply a cargo of coal to a third party, X, or to anyone X nominated. Scotson was instructed by X to deliver the coal to Pegg, and Pegg promised to unload the coal at a stated rate of pay. He subsequently failed to do the agreed unloading. Scotson sued Pegg, claiming that their promise to deliver coal to him was consideration for his promise to unload it. Pegg claimed that this could not be consideration, since Scotson was already bound to supply the coal under the contract with X. The court upheld Scotson's claim: delivery of the coal was consideration because it was a benefit to Pegg, and a detriment to Scotson in that it prevented them from having the option of breaking their contract with X.

Waiver and Promissory estoppel

These are ways of making some kind of promise binding even where there is no consideration. Waiver has traditionally applied where one party agrees not to enforce their strict rights under the contract by, for example, accepting delivery later than agreed. One case that illustrates the doctrine of waiver is that of Hickman v Haynes (1875). A buyer asked the seller to deliver goods later than originally agreed and then when the delivery was made refused to accept it. The seller sued for breach of contract, the buyer responded by arguing that the seller was in breach, for delivering later than specified. The courts rejected the buyer's argument on the grounds that the delivery was made at the buyer's request.

Promissory estoppel (stopping the contract on the basis of a promise) is a newer doctrine than waiver, developing the concept. It was introduced by Lord Denning in the Central London Property Trust Ltd v High Trees (1947) where owners of a block of flats had promised to accept reduced rents in 1939. There was no consideration for their promise but Lord Denning nevertheless stated that he would estop them from recovering any arrears. He based his case on the decision in Hughes v Metropolitan Railways (1875). In this case, under the lease the tenants were obliged to keep the premises in good repair, and in October 1874, the landlord gave them six months notice to do some repairs stating that if they were not done in time, the lease would be forfeited. In November the two parties began to negotiate the possibility of the tenants buying the lease, the tenants stating in the meantime that they would not carry out the repairs. By December the negotiations had broken down and at the end of the six-month notice period, the landlord claimed that the lease was forfeited because the tenants had not done the repairs. The House of Lords (now Supreme Court) held however, that the landlord's conduct was an implied promise to the tenants that he would not enforce the forfeiture at the end of the notice period, and in not doing the repairs, the tenants had been relying on this premise. It was seen that the six-month notice period began again when negotiations broke down.

The exact scope of the doctrine is a matter of debate, but certain requirements must be met:

- Estoppel only applies to the modification of discharge of an existing contractual obligation. It cannot create a new contract.
- It can only be used as a 'shield' and not a 'sword'.
- The promise not to enforce rights must be clear and unequivocal.
- It must be inequitable for the promisor to go back on his promise.
- The promisee must have acted in reliance on the promise, although not necessarily to his detriment.

Agreement by deed

Land law, The Law of Property Miscellaneous Provisions Act1989, requires all transfers of land or the creation of interests in land, such as gifts or mortgages, to be made by way of legal deed, otherwise it is void as far as the legal estate is concerned. A document will be a deed if:

- It makes clear on the face of it that it is intended to be a deed;
- It is validly executed as a deed by all those required to sign it;
- It is validly executed as a deed by an individual if it is signed by the individual in the presence of a witness who attests to the signature, or at their direction and in their presence and the presence of two witnesses who each attest the signature, and it is delivered as a deed by them or a person authorised to do so on their behalf.

When is the transfer deed fully effective?

In registered land, the transfer deed is legally effected only when it is lodged at the Land Registry for registration on the official Registered Title of the property. If the transfer is of unregistered land, the transfer deed is effective immediately to vest the legal estate in the purchaser, but the transfer must be lodged for first registration of title with the Land Registry within 2 months (otherwise the seller will hold the legal estate on bare trust for the purchaser). However, the 2-month period can be extended with good reason.

Rights that are overreaching

A purchaser will take the property subject to the beneficial interests of anyone they knew or ought to have known about (under the doctrine of 'notice'). A typical example is where the purchaser buys land subject to a trust, knowing that an individual has a life interest in the property and can remain in occupation until their death.

Overreaching is a process whereby the beneficiaries' equitable interests are effectively dissolved and lifted from the land, and then attached to the purchase price. The purchaser then takes the land free from the beneficiaries' equitable interests, whether or not he knew or ought to have known of them, and the beneficiary claims his entitlement from the money made through the selling of the property.

When does overreaching apply?

Overreaching is capable of applying only to the equitable interests listed in section 2 Law of Property Act 1925. These are generally those existing behind a trust and having a monetary value. Section 2(1) LPA 1925 provides that: "A conveyance to a purchaser of a legal estate in land shall overreach any equitable interest or power affecting that estate [and listed in the section] whether or not he has notice thereof."

Generally speaking, for overreaching to be effective the purchaser (which includes a mortgagee) must pay the purchase money/mortgage loan to all of the trustees (at least two, or a trust corporation). Provided this is done, the purchaser/mortgagee takes free of any beneficial interests existing behind a trust. The beneficiaries' equitable interests are then lifted from the land and automatically attached to the money paid by the purchaser (i.e. to the proceeds of sale).

****

1.3
Terms of Contracts

Once a contract has been formed, it is necessary to define the scope of the obligations which each party incurs. Terms of contracts describe the respective duties and obligations of each party to the contract. As well as the contractual terms laid out and agreed by parties to a contract, called express terms, there may also be implied terms – terms that are 'read into' a contract because of the facts of the agreement and the apparent intention of the parties or the law on specific types of contract.

Express terms of contract

Oral statements

In all transactions, with the exception of the simplest, there will be some negotiations before a contract is made. These are usually oral statements or based on oral statements. Problems can arise following oral statements when parties cannot agree whether the statement was intended to be binding. In considering questions such as these a court will classify statements made during negotiations as either representations or terms. A representation is a statement that may have encouraged one of the parties to make the contract, but is not itself part of the contract, while a term is an undertaking that is part of the contract.

Representation can also be construed as misrepresentation, which is a common cause of dispute. Whether a statement is either a representation or a term is mainly a question of the party's intentions.

If the parties have indicated that a particular statement is a term of their contract, then the court will carry out that intention.

Written terms of a contract

Written terms can be incorporated into a contract in three different ways: by signature, by reasonable notice and by a previous course of dealing.

The parol evidence rule

Under this rule, where there is a written contract, extrinsic (parol) evidence cannot change the express terms laid down in that document. Extrinsic evidence includes oral statements and written material such as draft contracts or letter, whether relating to pre-contract negotiations or the parties post contractual behavior. One case that illustrates the parol evidence rule is Henderson v Arthur (1907). The plaintiffs and the defendant were parties to a lease that contained a covenant for the payment of rent quarterly in advance, although before the lease was drawn up the parties agreed that the rent could be paid in arrears. When the tenant was sued for not paying quarterly in advance, he pointed out this prior agreement. The court held that the terms of prior oral agreement could not be substituted for the terms of a later formal contract covering the same transaction. There are a few exceptions to the parol evidence rule, the following being the main ones:

Rectification

Where a document is intended to record a previous oral agreement but fails to do that accurately, evidence of the oral agreement will be admitted.

Partially written agreements

Where there is a written agreement, but the parties clearly intended it to be qualified by other written or oral statements, the parol evidence rule is displaced.

Implied terms

The parol evidence rule only applies where a party seeks to use existing evidence to alter the express terms of a contract. Where a contract is of a type that is unusually subject to terms implied by law and statute, parol evidence may be given to support, or to deny, the usual implication.

Collateral agreements

There is a way in which an oral statement can be deemed binding, even though it conflicts with a written contract and does not fall within any of the exceptions to the parol rule. If one party says something like 'I will sign this document if you will assure me that it means....' The courts may find that two contracts have been created, the written agreement and a collateral contract based on the oral statement.

Construction of express terms in contracts

The courts will sometimes have to determine the construction of an express term within a contract. The courts will have to 'seek the meaning which the document would convey to a reasonable person having all the background knowledge which would have reasonably been available to parties at the time of entering into the agreement'. The courts start by presuming that the parties meant what they said. The courts would also look at the outcome of the words and meaning to see if they create an absurdity or are inconsistent with the rest of the contract.

Implied terms

As well as the express terms laid down in the contract, further terms may be sometimes read into the contract by the courts. These implied terms are divided into four groups: terms implied by fact, terms implied by law, terms implied by custom and terms implied by trade usage. Terms implied by fact are terms not laid out in the contract, but which it is assumed both parties would have intended to include if they had thought about it, they may have left them out by mistake. In order to decide what the intention of the parties was, the courts have developed two tests, the 'officious bystander test, and the 'business efficacy' test.

The officious bystander test was laid down in Shirlaw v Southern Foundries (1926). The Judge said, ...'that which in any contract is left to be implied and need not be expressed is something so obvious that it goes without saying: so that, if while the parties were making their bargain, an officious bystander were to suggest some express provision for it in the agreement, they would testily suppress him with a common 'oh, of course'. The business efficacy test covers terms which one side alleges must be implied to make the contract work, to give it business efficacy.

Terms implied by law are terms which the law dictates must be present in certain types of contract-in some cases whether the parties intended them or not.

In Liverpool Council v Irwin (1977) the defendants lived in a council maisonette that was part of a high-rise block in Liverpool. The block was in a bad condition and tenants withheld rent and the case went to court with the tenants arguing that the council was in breach of contract (tenancy). The council argued that there was no agreement to keep the block in good condition and the courts argued that good

45

repair and safety were implied terms of contract. The council lost the case.

implied terms may arise from contracts governing the supply of goods and services, such as the Consumer Rights Act 2015. Terms implied by custom can be implied into a contract if there is evidence that under local custom they would normally be there.

Terms implied by trade usage would normally be part of a contract made by parties in a particular trade or business.

The classification of contractual terms

There are three types of contractual terms, conditions, warranties and innominate terms. A condition is a term that the courts would regard as important in that it would clearly have negative consequences if breached.

Where a condition is breach the injured party can regard the contract as repudiated, and need not render any further performance, and can also sue for damages.

Warranties denote contractual terms that can be broken without highly important consequences. This would be a minor term and would not entitle the party to terminate the contract it merely entitles him to sue. The Consumer Rights Act 2015 designates certain terms as warranties breach of which does not allow the buyer to treat the contract as discharged, but merely to sue for damages, for example, the right to quiet enjoyment.

One such case that illustrates the above is that of Bettini v Gye (1876) where a singer was engaged to sing for a whole season and to arrive six days in advance to take part in rehearsals. He arrived only three days in advance. It was held that the rehearsal clause was a warranty, as it was subsidiary to the main clause. The management were therefore not entitled to treat the contract as discharged. They should have kept to the original contract and sought damages for the three days delay.

Innominate terms are terms that can be broken with either important or trivial consequences, depending on the nature of the breach.

Innominate terms were illustrated in Hong Kong Fir Shipping Co Ltd v Kawasaki Kisen Kaisha (1962) in which the defendants had chartered a ship for two years from the claimants. Twenty weeks of the charter were lost due to condition of ship and incompetent staff. The agreement contained a clause stating that the ship was 'in every way fitted for ordinary cargo service'. There was no doubt that the defendants were entitled to bring an action for damages but instead decided to terminate the contract. The claimants counter sued, claiming that the breach did not entitle the defendants to terminate, only to claim damages. The Court of Appeal agreed, stating that the question to be asked was that whether as a result of the breach the defendants had been deprived of the whole of the benefit of the contract. As this was not the case, the termination was unjustified.

Unfair contract terms

Contract terms can be considered to be so unfair to one of the contracting parties that the courts have had to intervene to prevent an injustice. This has usually arisen within the context of exemption clauses and is controlled both by common law and the exemption clauses in contracts. Parts 1 and 2 of the Consumer Rights Act 2015 consolidate and replace the Unfair Terms in Consumer Contracts Regulations 1999 (UTCCRs) and relevant provisions of the Unfair Contract Terms Act 1977 (UCTA).

The Unfair Contract Terms Act 1977 applies only to exemption clauses covering business liability and, since the CRA 2015, does not cover any exemption clauses that would be covered by the Act, i.e. in contracts between a trader and a consumer. The Act defines a 'trader' as a person acting for purposes relating to that persons trade, business craft or profession. A 'consumer' is defined as an individual acting for purposes that are wholly or mainly outside the indiviual's trade, business, craft or profession (see Overy v Paypal (Europe) Ltd 2012.

In certain cases, one party to a contract may seek to avoid incurring liabilities for breach of contract, or may specify that their liability for such a breach will be limited, usually to a specific amount of damages. However, a clause that seeks to exclude all liability for uncertain breaches is called an exclusion clause. There are many examples such as holiday companies seeking to exclude all liability for holidays gone wrong or cancelled. Over the past 40 years the law has sought to control the use of these clauses, first by the efforts of judges and also by legislation such as the Unfair Contract Terms Act 1977 and the Unfair Terms in Consumer Contracts Regulations 1999, now consolidated as described above by the CRA 2015.

Misrepresentation in contracts

Even in cases where a contract clearly meets the requirements of offer and acceptance, consideration and intent to create legal relations, it will still not be binding if, at the time the contract was made, certain factors were present which meant that there was no genuine concern. These are known as vitiating factors (because they vitiate, or invalidate, consent). The vitiating factors that the law recognizes as preventing a contract are misrepresentation, mistake, duress, undue influence and illegality. In these cases, the innocent party may set the contract aside if he wishes. If one party has been induced to enter into a contract by a statement made by the other party, and that statement is untrue, the contract is voidable and the innocent party may also be able to claim damages. For a misrepresentation to be actionable it must be untrue, a statement of fact not opinion, and it must have induced the innocent party to enter into the contract.

It is worth noting that, following the amendments to the Consumer Protection from Unfair Trading Regulations 2008 (CPRs 2008) made by the Consumer Protection Amendment Regulations 2014, after October 1st 2014 consumers who entered into a contract for the sale or supply of a product by a trader or who entered into a contract to sell a product to a trader (for example selling a car to a dealer) or made a payment to a trader for the supply of a product, and that trader engaged in a prohibited practice in relation to that product, for example by giving misleading information, have an extended range of specific consumer 'rights to redress' under the CPRs (right to unwind, right to a discount, and specific rights to damages). This regime is separate to the consumers general remedies but the consumer cannot make a claim twice for the same product. In addition, there is an amendment to s.2 of the Misrepresentation Act 1967 which removes the ability of consumers to recover damages under that legislation where they have a right to redress under the CPRs in respect of the misrepresentation,

There are four different types of misrepresentation, fraudulent misrepresentation, where there is clear deceit, negligent, where misrepresentation arises through acts of negligence but not deceit and innocent misrepresentation which is not fraudulent but is still clear misrepresentation. The effect of a misrepresentation is generally to make a contract voidable, rather than void, so the contract will continue to exist unless or until the injured party chooses to have it set aside by the courts by means of rescission. Rescission is an equitable remedy that sets the contract aside and puts the parties back in the position where they were before the misrepresentation. An injured party who decides to rescind the contract may do so by notifying the other party or, if this is not possible owing to the conduct of the party, by taking some reasonable action to indicate the intention to default. A case that illustrates this is Car and Universal Finance Co Ltd v Caldwell (1965) where the defendant sold and delivered a car and was paid by cheque. The cheque bounced, by which time the car and buyer had disappeared. The defendant notified the police and the Automobile Association. While the police were investigating the buyer sold the car to a dealer who knew that the car was not the buyer's to sell. Finally, the car dealer sold the car to the claimants who bought it in good faith. The court of Appeal held that by contacting the police and the AA the claimant had made his intention to rescind the contract clear. As soon as this happened the ownership of the car reverted to him. This meant that at the time the car was sold back to the claimant the car was not anyone's to sell.

Another case illustrating this is Whittington v Seale-Hayne (1900) where the plaintiff's, breeders of prize poultry, were induced to take a lease of the defendant's premises by his innocent representation that the premises were in a sanitary condition. Under the lease, the plaintiff's covenanted to execute any works required by any local or public authority. Owing to the insanitary conditions of the premises, the water supply was poisoned, the plaintiff's manager and his family became very ill, and the poultry became valueless for breeding purposes or died.

The court rescinded the lease, and held that the plaintiffs could recover an indemnity for what they had spent on rates, rent and repairs under the covenants in the lease, because these expenses arose necessarily out of the contract. It refused to award compensation for other leases, since to do so would be to award damages, not an indemnity, there being no obligation created by the contract to carry on a poultry farm on the premises or to employ a manager, etc.

Representation and terms of a contract

Section 1 of the Misrepresentation Act 1967, s.2 as amended by The Consumer Protection Amendment Regulations 2014, described above, provides that where a misrepresentation becomes a term of the contract, the innocent party may bring an action for both misrepresentation and breach of contract. Under section 3 of this Act, as amended by the Unfair Contract Terms Act 1977, as amended by the CRA 2015, exemption clauses that attempt to exclude or limit liability for misrepresentations are operative only if reasonable. This provision is illustrated in Walker v Boyle (1982) where the seller of a house told the buyer that there were no disputes regarding the boundaries of the property. This was not true. This misrepresentation appeared to entitle the buyer to rescind the contract and notwithstanding a clause seeking to deny this, the court granted a rescission.

Mistake

The general rule is that a mistake has no effect on a contract, but certain mistakes of a fundamental nature, sometimes called operative mistakes, may render a contract void at common law. If the contract is rendered void, then the parties will be returned to their original positions, and this may defeat the rights of innocent third parties who may have acquired an interest in the contract.

The reluctance of the courts to develop the common law doctrine of mistake is probably due to the unfortunate consequences for third parties that can result from holding a contract void. Equity at one stage intervened to create a more flexible doctrine, but this has been overruled. We discuss mistakes in more depth in the next chapter.

Rectification

Where there has been a mistake, not in the actual agreement but in reducing it in writing, equity will order rectification of the document so that it coincides with the true agreement of the parties. The main conditions for this are that:

- The document does not represent the intention of both parties; or
- One party mistakenly believes that a term was included in the document and the other party knew of this error.
- There must have been a concluded agreement but not necessarily an enforceable contract. Rectification is an equitable remedy and is available at the discretion of the court.

Refusal of specific performance

Specific performance will be refused when the contract is void at common law. Equity may also refuse specific performance where a contract is valid at law, but only 'where a hardship amounting to injustice would have been inflicted upon him by holding him to his bargain' (Tamplin v James (1879)).

Duress

This requires actual or threatened violence to the person. Originally, it was the only form of duress recognized by the law. This is highlighted by the case of Barton v Armstrong (1975) where a managing director was threatened with death if he did not purchase a former chairman's shares. The managing director was happy to purchase the shares notwithstanding the threats that had been made. It was held that the threats constituted duress and the contract was set aside. We will look at duress in more depth in chapter 7.

****

1.4

Contracts And Illegality

Although a contract, on the face of it may contain all the elements of a valid agreement, such as offer and consideration, that contract may still be legally unenforceable. Contracts may be illegal at the time of their formation or because of the way they have been performed. A contract may be illegal when entered into because the contract cannot be performed in accordance with its terms without committing an illegal act. For example, a contract may involve a breach of the criminal law, or it may be a statutory requirement for the parties to the contract to have a license that they in fact do not have. A case that illustrates this is Levy v Yates (1838). In this case, there existed a statutory rule that a royal license was required to perform a play within 20 miles of London. In that case the contract was between a theatre owner and an impresario for the performance of a theatrical production where no royal license had been obtained. The contract was thus illegal at the time of its formation.

Illegal mode of performance
In some cases a contract may be perfectly legal when it was made, but may be carried out in an illegal manner. A case that illustrates this is Anderson Ltd v Daniel (1924). In this case, a statute provided that a seller of artificial fertilizer had to supply buyers with an invoice detailing certain chemicals used in its manufacture. The sellers failed to provide the invoice needed. Although not against the law to sell fertilizer it was against statutory rules not to supply an invoice. As a

result the sellers were unable to claim the price when the defendants refused to pay. A contract is obviously illegal if it involves a contravention of the law. However, a contract is also regarded as being illegal where it involves conduct that the law disapproves of as contrary to the interests of the public, even though the conduct is not actually unlawful. In both cases the transaction is treated as an illegal contract and the courts will not enforce it.

Contracts violating legal rules
Breach of common law

There are a number of factors that may make a contract illegal at common law, the most important where there is a contract to commit a crime or tort (negligent act). These are obvious breaches of the law. However, another very important area is contracts in restraint of trade. The issue of restraint of trade commonly arises and concerns those contracts that limit an individuals right to use their skills for payment, or to trade freely. These contracts fall into four groups:

- Contracts for the sale of a business where the vendor promises not to compete with the purchaser
- Contracts between businesses by which prices or output are regulated
- Contracts in which an employee agrees that on leaving employment they will not set up in business or be employed in such as way as to compete with their employer or ex employer. This is most common in business where personal skills and reputation attract custom, such as advertising and the ex-employee may take with them valuable customers
- Contracts where a person agrees to restrict their mode of trade by, for example, only accepting orders from one particular

company. This is sometimes called a 'solus' agreement and is frequently used for petrol stations, in return for the land or lease the trader promises to use the product of the seller (Esso Petroleum v Harper's Garage (Stourport) 1968).

Any of the above can be held to create a restraint of trade, a general restraint if the contract completely prohibits trading, or a partial restraint if it limits trading to a certain time or area.

Breach of legislation

Some types of contract are expressly declared void by statute. The two most important examples of contracts that are expressly declared void by statute are contracts in constraint of trade and wagering contracts.

Contracts in restraint of trade

As stated above, these are arrangements by which one party agrees to limit his or her legal right to carry out a trade, business or profession. A contract that does this is always viewed as *prima facie* void for two reasons:

- To prevent people signing away their livelihoods at the request of a party with stronger bargaining power
- To avoid depriving the public of the person's expertise.

These contracts are of several possible types as mentioned above-employee restraints, vendor restraints-preventing the seller of a business from unfairly competing with the purchaser and agreements of mutual regulation between businesses. However, these agreements might be upheld as reasonable:

- as between the parties-so the restraint must be no wider than to protect a legitimate interest
- in the public interest-so the restraint must not unduly limit public choice.

The reasonableness of the restraint is also measured against factors such as duration and geographical extent.

Employee restraints

An employer can legitimately protect trade secrets and client connection, but not merely prevent the employee from exercising his or her trade or skill. Reasonableness is measured against certain criteria:

A restraint in a highly specialised business is more likely to be reasonable. In Forster and Sons Ltd v Suggett (1918) - court held that a restraint of 5 years on an employee from engaging in glass or glass bottle manufacturing was reasonable given the time and money invested into their training. Nordenfelt v Maxim Nordenfelt Guns and Ammunition Co Ltd (1894) - the court held that a term prohibiting Nordenfelt from starting a competing business anywhere in the world for 25 years was reasonable.

Pursuant to the Nordenfelt principle, restraint of trade clauses are void and unenforceable unless they are reasonable by reference to the interests of the parties and the public. The restraint must also be reasonable in terms of time and space. 3 Restraint of an employee in a key position is more likely to be reasonable.

An employer is not entitled to protect itself against the use of the skill and knowledge which the employee acquired during his or her employment. Those belong to the employee, who must be free to exploit them in the market place. Neither can an employer seek protection from competition per se since it is against the public interest that employees should be deprived of the opportunity to earn their living or to use their personal skills to the ultimate benefit of the community as a whole:

Herbert Morris Limited v Saxelby
[1916] AC 688.

Instead the employer must demonstrate that the covenant protects a legitimate business interest. In the Herbert Morris case, Lord Parker defined this as "some proprietary right, whether in the nature of a trade connection or in the nature of trade secrets, for the protection of which such a restraint is reasonably necessary". The concept was further developed by Lord Wilberforce in Stenhouse Australia Limited v Phillips [1974] 1 All ER 117, who said:

"The employer's claim for protection must be based on the identification of some advantage or asset inherent in the business which can properly be regarded as, in a general sense, his property, and which it would be unjust to allow the employee to appropriate for his own purposes, even though he (the employee) may have contributed to its creation".

In other words, the employer is entitled to prevent the employee taking unfair advantage of confidential information and business connections to which he had access in the course of his/her employment.

An employee may be significant to the business without even being a member of staff as demonstrated in Leeds rugby Ltd v Harris (2005).

The duration of the extent must not be too long (Home Counties Dairies v Skilton (1970) and the geographical extent too wide (Fitch v Dewes (1921). Similarly, the range of activities that the restraint covers must be no wider than is necessary to protect legitimate interests (J A Mont (UK) Ltd v Mills (1993).

Soliciting of clients can be prevented by such clauses, if not too wide (M&S Drapers v Reynolds (1957). Also, including clients not within the original scope of the restraint is not unreasonable (Hanover Insurance Brokers Ltd and Christchurch Insurance Brokers Ltd v Shapiro (1994). Attempting a restraint by other means is also void, including making contractual benefits subject to a restraint (Bull v Pitney Bowes Ltd (1966) and restraints in rules of associations (Eastham v Newcastle United FC Ltd (1963).

Vendor restraints
These are void for public policy to prevent an individual from negotiating away his or her livelihood and also because the public may lose a valuable service. Restraints are more likely to be upheld as reasonable since businesses deal on more equal bargaining strength, even is restraint is very wide (Nordenfelt v Maxim Nordenfelt Co (1894).

The restraint must still protect a legitimate interest to be valid (British Concrete Ltd v Schelff (1921).

Agreements between merchants, manufacturers or other trades
If the object is regulation of trade then they are void unless both sides benefit (English Hop Growers v Dering (1928). So they are void when the parties have unequal bargaining strength (Schroder Publishing Co Ltd v Macaulay (1974)-unless public policy dictates otherwise: Panayiotou v Sony Music International (UK) Ltd (1994).

Wagering contracts

Wagering agreements are bets, and were rendered void by The Gaming Act 1845 which remained in force until the Gambling Act 2005, which came into force in stages to 2007. The Act provides:

"All contracts or agreements, whether by parole or in writing, by way of gaming or wagering, shall be null and void, and no suit shall be brought or maintained in a court of law or equity for recovering any sum of money or valuable thing alleged to be won upon any wager..."

The Act does not make wagering agreements illegal it simply provides that neither party to such an agreement can legally enforce it. For the provisions of the legislation to apply, a wagering contract must be one in which there are two parties and the terms of the agreement are such that one party wins and the other loses. This means that football pools, for example, are not covered as its promoters take a percentage of the stake money and so gain by the transaction regardless of whether players win as well. The Act also covers gaming, which is defined by the Betting, Gaming and lotteries act 1963 as 'the playing of a game of chance for winnings in money or money's worth'. Games of chance include games that depend partly on skill and partly on chance. Athletic games and sports are excluded.

Competition law

Common law lays down certain controls on contracts in constraint of trade. These controls give only limited protection and actual legislation provides more adequate protection. One of the main goals of the European Union, through Article 85, is to promote free trade between member states and clearly restrictive trade can affect this policy. Where a restrictive trade agreement could affect trade between member states it will only be valid if allowed under both EU and English law.

In terms of contracts in English law, the relevant legislation is now contained in the Competition Act 1998 Along with the Enterprise Act 2002. This Act prohibits a number of anti-competitive practices. The 1998 Act applies to agreements between undertakings, decisions by associations of undertakings or concerted practices that (a) may affect trade and (b) have as their object or effect the prevention, restriction or distortion of trade. For the Act to prohibit an agreement the effect of the agreement must be significant and not minor.

Contracts against public policy

There exist a wide-range of contracts that are considered to be illegal because they are against public policy. As we discussed, public policy really means the interest of society at large and the contract must contravene it. Contracts promoting sexual immorality for example are seen as contravening public policy.

One case that illustrates this is Armhouse Lee Ltd v Chappell (1996) concerning a contract under which the defendants paid the plaintiffs to place adverts for telephone sex lines in magazines. When regulation concerning such publicity was tightened the defendants terminated the contract, as they no longer wished to advertise their services in this way. The plaintiffs brought an action for the money due under the contract and the defendants argued that the contract was illegal and unenforceable as it promoted sexual immorality. This defense was rejected by the Court of Appeal. The court held that though the adverts were distasteful the sex lines were generally accepted by society and were regulated by the telephone industry. There was no evidence, in the eyes of the Court of Appeal that any 'generally accepted moral code' condemned these telephone sex lines. It considered that contracts should only be found illegal under this heading if an element of public harm clearly existed.

Contracts prejudicial to public safety

The main types of contracts found illegal on these grounds are contracts with those living in an enemy country, contracts to perform acts which are illegal in a friendly foreign country and contracts which are damaging to foreign relations.

The effect of an illegal contract

The effect of an illegal contract will depend on whether it is illegal due to a statute or due to the common law. Where the contract is illegal due to a statute, in some cases the statute provides for the consequences of any illegality. Under common law an illegal contract is void and courts will not order it to be performed. The precise effects of an illegal contract depend on whether the contract is illegal at the time of formation or is illegal due to the way in which it was performed.

Contracts illegal at the time of formation are treated as if they were never made, so the illegal contract is unenforceable by either party. Contracts illegal as performed are slightly different as to their effect. It will be possible to enforce the illegal contract if the illegal act was merely incidental to the performance of the contract. For example, a contract for the delivery of goods may not be tainted by illegality when the lorry driver is caught speeding or under the influence of drink. Where the contract is merely illegal because of the way it was performed, it is possible for either both or only one of the parties to intend illegal performance. If both parties are aware that a contracts performance is illegal, the consequences for this type of contract are the same as for a contract that was illegal at the time of its formation. When one party did not know of the illegal performance of the contract by the other party, the innocent party can enforce it. In some cases, it is possible to divide the illegal part of a contract from the rest and enforce the provisions which are not affected by the illegality-this is called severance. The illegal parts of the contract can be severed if they are relatively unimportant to the contract and if the severance leaves the nature of the contract unaltered.

****

1.5

Discharge of a Contract

A contract is said to be discharged when the rights and obligations in it come to an end. There are four ways in which a contract can come to an end: performance under the contract, i.e., natural end, end by mutual agreement, breach of contract and frustration. We should look at these areas in turn.

Performance under contract

This is the most obvious way of parties discharging their obligations and bringing the contract to a satisfactory end. In many cases, it is uncomplicated but there are some cases where one party may claim to have discharged their obligations and the other party disagrees. The law then has to look at the question of what constitutes performance. The obvious and general rule is that performance must exactly match the requirements laid down in the contract. This is known as entire performance. If the first party fails to perform then the other party need pay nothing at all, even if the shortfall actually causes no hardship. This is the simple rule and obviously contracts can be more complicated, with claim and counter claim. The case of Cutter v Powell (1795) demonstrates the difficulty. A sailor had contracted to serve on a ship traveling from Jamaica to Liverpool. He was to be paid 30 Guineas for the voyage, payable when the ship arrived in Liverpool. However, he died during the journey. His widow sued for wages up until he died, but her claim was unsuccessful, as the court held that the contract required entire performance.

Similarly, in Bolton v Mahadeva (1972) a central heating system gave out less heat than it should, and there were fumes in one room. It was held that the contractor could not claim payment; although the boiler and pipes had been installed, they did not fulfill the primary purpose of heating the house.

The rule can also allow parties to escape from what has become an unprofitable contract to do so by taking advantage of the most minor departures from its terms. In Re Moore and Co Ltd and Landaur and Co (1921) the contract concerned the sale of canned fruit that were to be packed into cases of 30 tins. On delivery it was discovered that although the correct number of tins had been sent, almost half the cases contained only 24 tins in each. This made no difference to the market value of the goods, but the buyers pointed out that the sale was covered by the Sale of Goods Act, which stated that goods sold by description must correspond with that description. The delivery did not, and the buyers were within their rights to reject the whole consignment.

Mitigation of the entire performance rule

Substantial performance
This doctrine allows a party who has performed with only minor defects to claim the price of the work done, less any money the other party will have to spend to put the defects right.

Severable contracts
A contract is said to be severable where payment becomes due at various stages of performance, rather than in one lump sum when performance is complete. Most contracts of employment are examples of this. Also, major building contracts also operate in this way, allowing

for stage payments. In a severable contract the money due at the end of each stage may be claimed and the person carrying out the work under the contract can refuse to continue if the payments are not made.

Prevention of performance by one party

Where one party performs one part of the agreed obligation, and is then prevented from completing the rest of the contract because of a fault of the other party, a quantum meruit can be claimed from the other party. Quantum meruit is an assessment of the amount performed to date and a reasonable price arrived at.

Breach of terms concerning time

The judgment here will be that of an assessment of whether 'time is of the essence' and the effect that completing the contract out of time has on the other party.

Frustration of contract

The basic principle underlying frustration of contract is that, after a contract is made, something happens, through no fault of the parties own, to make fulfillment of the contract impossible. Although there are many situations that can make it impossible to fulfill a contract only certain cases can be seen as genuine frustration. When a contract is discharged by frustration both parties are excused performance of their future obligations and the application of the Law Reform (Frustrated Contracts) Act 1943 determines what happens to advance payments (such as deposits and any other payments due) made before the frustrating event and claims for reimbursement for contractual expenses and performance conferred prior to frustration.

The modern doctrine of frustration arose from Taylor v Caldwell (1863). The parties in the case had entered into an agreement concerning the use of Surrey Gardens and music hall for a series of concerts and day and night fetes. Six days before the planned date for the first concert, the building was burnt down, making it impossible for the concerts to go ahead. The party planning to put on the concerts was sued for breach of contract but the action failed, as fulfillment of the contract was impossible.

The concept and practice of frustration of contract can be placed in three categories: events that make performance or further performance impossible; events that make performance illegal; and those that make it pointless.

Impossible to fulfill contract

A contract may become impossible to perform because of destruction or unavailability of something essential for the contract to be performed.

Death of either party to the contract

Unavailability of party. Contracts which require personal performance will be frustrated if one party, for example, is ill or is imprisoned, providing that the non-availability of the party substantially effects performance

Method of performance impossible

Where a contract lays down a particular method of performance and this becomes impossible, the contract may be frustrated. A contract is unlikely to be frustrated simply because performance has become more expensive or more onerous than expected.

The leading modern case on frustration is Davis Contractors Co Ltd v Fareham UDC (1956). Davis, a construction company contracted to build 78 houses for a local authority. The job was to take eight months, at a price of £94,000. In fact, labor shortages delayed the work, which ended up taking 22 months and cost the builders £22,000 more than they had planned for. The defendant was willing to pay the contract price in spite of the delay, but Davis sought to have the contract discharged on the grounds of frustration arguing that labor shortages made performance fundamentally different from that envisaged in the contract (it intended to seek payment on a quantum meruit basis to cover costs).

However, the House of Lords decided that the events that caused the delays were within the range of changes that could reasonably be expected to happen during the performance of a contract for building houses and the change of circumstances did not make performance radically different from what was expected. Therefore, the contract was not frustrated. Lord Radcliffe explained:

'it is not hardship or inconvenience or material loss which itself calls the principle of frustration into play. There must be as well such a change in the significance of the obligation that the thing undertaken would, if performed, be different from that contracted for'.

Illegality

If, after a contract is formed, a change in the law makes its performance illegal, the contract will be frustrated.

Performance made pointless

A contract can be frustrated where a supervening event makes performance of a contract completely pointless, though still technically possible. A contract can be rendered pointless if there has been such a drastic change of circumstances as to dramatically alter the nature of the contract.

Time of frustrating event

In order to frustrate a contract, the event in question must occur after the contract is made.

Limits to the doctrine of frustration

The doctrine of frustration will not be applied on the grounds of inconvenience, increase in expense or loss of profit. The case above that highlights this is Davis Contractors Limited v Fareham UDC (1956). It will also not apply where there is express provision in the contract covering the intervening event or where the frustration is self-induced.

A contract will not be frustrated if the event making performance impossible was the voluntary action of one party. If the party concerned had a choice open to him, and chose to act as to make performance impossible, then frustration will be self induced and the court will refuse to treat the contract as discharged.

One such case that highlights this is The Superservant Two (1990). In this case one of the two barges owned by the defendants and used to transport oil rigs was sunk. They were therefore unable to fulfill their contract to transport an oil rig belonging to the plaintiff as their other barge (superservant one) was already allocated to other contracts. It was held that the contract was not frustrated. The defendants had another barge available, but chose not to allocate it to the contract with the plaintiffs.

Where the event was foreseeable

If, by reason of special knowledge, the event was foreseeable by one party, then he cannot claim frustration. This was highlighted in

Amalgamated Investment and Property Co v John Walker and Sons Ltd (1976) where the possibility that a building could be listed was foreseen by the plaintiff who had enquired about the matter beforehand. A failure to obtain planning permission was also foreseeable and was a normal risk for property developers. The contract was therefore not frustrated.

Breach of contract

A contract is breached when one party performs defectively, or differently from the agreement or not at all (actual breach) or indicates in advance that they will not be performing as agreed (anticipatory breach). Where an anticipatory breach occurs, the other party can sue for breach straight away, it is not necessary to wait until performance falls due. One case illustrating this is Frost v Knight (1872) where the defendant had promised to marry the plaintiff once his father had died. He later broke off the engagement before his father died, and when his ex fiancé sued him for breach of promise, he argued that she had no claim as the time for performance had not yet arrived. This argument was rejected and the plaintiff's case succeeded. Any effect of a breach of contract will entitle the innocent party to sue for damages but not every breach will entitle the wronged party to discharge the contract. If the contract is not discharged it will still need to be performed.

There are three main circumstances where the innocent party may wish to seek to discharge the contract:

Repudiation – this is where one party makes it clear that they no longer wish to be bound by the contract, either during its performance or before performance is due

Breach of a condition – Breach of a condition allows the innocent party to terminate the contract.

Serious breach of an innominate term- where the relevant term is classified as innominate, it will be the one that can be breached in both serious and trivial ways, and whether the innocent party is entitled to terminate or not will depend on how serious the results of the breach are. If the results are so serious as to undermine the foundations of the contract, the innocent party will have the right to terminate.

Even when one of these three types of breach occurs, the contract is not automatically discharged. The innocent party can usually choose whether or not to terminate. If the innocent party chooses to terminate this must be clearly communicated to the other party.

Agreement

In some cases, the parties to a contract will simply agree to terminate the contract, so that one or both parties are released from their obligations. A distinction is usually made between bilateral discharge where both parties will benefit from the ending by agreement and a unilateral discharge where one party benefits. In general an agreed discharge will be binding if it contains the same elements that make a contract binding when it is formed. Those that present the most problems are formality and consideration.

Consideration

Consideration is not usually a problem where both parties agree to alter their obligations since each is giving something in return for the change. Problems are most likely to occur when one parties obligations change. If the other party agrees to the change, their agreement will only be binding if put into the form of a deed, or supported by consideration. Where consideration is provided in return for one party's agreement to change this is called 'accord'. The provision of consideration is called 'satisfaction'. The arrangement is often termed accord and satisfaction.

Formalities

This issue arises in connection with certain types of contract (mainly concerning the sale of land) that must be evidenced in writing to be binding under the Law of Property Act (1925).

Remedies for breach of contract

There are a number of remedies available to the innocent party in the event of a breached contract. There are two main remedies, those under common law and equitable remedies. There is a third category that involves remedies arising from the party's own agreement.

****

Ch.2

Business Law-Negligence and Duty of Care-General

In everyday parlance, negligence means a failure to pay attention to what ought to be done or to take the required level of care. Whereas its everyday usage implies a state of mind, the tort of negligence is concerned with the link between the defendant's behaviour and the risk that should have been foreseen.

Key definition of negligence

Negligence, as a tort, is generally defined as a breach of a duty of care. This duty of care is owed by one person to another. When damage is caused to a person, who then becomes a claimant, the type of damage has to be specified and also defined as actionable.

The loss or damage can arise in a number of ways, arising through misfeasance or nonfeasance and can consist of personal injury, damage to property or can be pure economic loss. It can also consist of psychiatric damage.

The duty of care-establishment of a duty

Certain relationships between people, recognised by the law and developed by the law, give rise to a legal duty of care. The following

Employer-employee

- Manufacturer to consumer

- Doctor-patient
- Solicitor-client

Essentially, carelessness by one party which affects another gives rise, or can give rise, to legal action by the injured party. It is up to the claimant to prove that damage has been caused and that the case falls into a specific situation that gives rise to a duty of care.

The neighbour principle
Donoghue v Stevenson 1932
Outside of the categories of established duty, a duty of care will be determined on the basis of individual circumstances.

One of the most prominent cases relating to Tort and negligence is that of *Donoghue v Stevenson* (HL 1932) In this case, Mrs Donoghue and friend visited a café and Mrs Donoghue's friend bought her a bottle of ginger beer. The bottle was made of opaque glass. When filling Mrs Donoghue's glass the remains of a decomposed a snail floated out of the bottle. Mrs Donoghue developed gastroenteritis as a result.

Mrs Donoghue brought an action against the manufacturer's of the ginger beer. Lord Atkin formulated a general principle in this case, the **neighbour principle**, for determining whether a duty of care should exist. He stated:

"You must take reasonable care to avoid acts or omissions which you can reasonably foresee would be likely to injure your neighbour. Who then, in law, is my neighbour? The answer seems to be persons who are so closely and directly affected by my act that I ought reasonably to have them in contemplation as being so affected when I am directing my mind to the acts or omissions which are called in question".

The manufacturers were found liable as they owed her a duty of care that the bottle did not contain foreign bodies which would damage her health.

This principle was a landmark and established negligence as an independent tort

Out of this judgement, which was further developed in the case of *Caparo Industries plc v Dickman* (1990), (which is further outlined below) also comes the concept of foresight, i.e. was the damage itself reasonably foreseeable. There must be a legal relationship of 'sufficient proximity' between the parties. There is also a requirement that it is 'just and reasonable' to impose a duty on the defendant.

Even where the courts are prepared to find that the circumstances are such as to be capable of giving rise to a duty of care, it is still likely that the claimant in a case could fail if he or she was an 'unforeseeable victim' of the defendants negligence.

One such case which amplifies this is *Bourhill v Young* (1943) where the plaintiff in the case heard, but did not actually see a crash caused by the motorcyclists (the defendants) negligence. The plaintiff later saw part of the aftermath of the accident and sued the defendant after suffering nervous shock, and lost the case, as harm to her of that type was not foreseeable.

Essentially, the legal proximity of claimant to defendant must be clearly established. In *Davis v Radcliffe* (1990), for example, Lord Goff stated that proximity referred to such a relation between the parties as rendered it just and reasonable that a duty should be imposed. Lack of proximity can, in some cases, be attributed to the failure of just and reasonable requirement in a case. A variety of factors are considered, such as the status of the parties and their relationship with one another, nature of injury or harm suffered and the particular way that the harm arises. One seminal case which further defined the boundaries of tort and negligence was that of *Hedley Byrne and Co v Heller and Partners Ltd* (1964). Lord Pearce observed:

"How wide the sphere of duty of care in negligence is to be laid depends primarily on the courts assessment of the demands of society for protection from the carelessness of others"

The case of Hedley Byrne concerned Economic loss through negligent information (see below).

Pure economic loss

Although financial loss incurred as a result of a negligent action against a person and property is normally recoverable, problems can arise with so called 'pure' economic loss, which is financial loss which has not been accompanied by any other damage. Cases of financial loss may arise as a result of either negligent information or advice, or of negligent conduct. In general, courts will assess these cases on a case-by-case basis, rather than rely purely on precedent.

Before the Hedley Byrne case, liability for negligent statements, or misstatements, which resulted in financial or other loss, existed in contract, in the tort of deceit or for breach of a fiduciary duty. In Hedley Byrne and Co v Heller and Partners Ltd the plaintiffs wanted to know if they could safely advance credit to their client, (A). The plaintiff's bankers sought references from the defendants (B) bankers, who gave favourable reports 'without responsibility'. The plaintiffs relied on the information and then suffered financial loss when A went into liquidation. In this case, it was held that no duty arose because of the disclaimer. However, importantly, in appropriate circumstances, a duty could arise.

It was accepted that reasonable foresight of the harm was not enough in itself, but that a 'special relationship' must exist where, to the defendants knowledge the plaintiff relied upon the defendants skill and judgement or his ability to make careful enquiry, and it was reasonable in the circumstances for the plaintiff to do so. The essence of Hedley and Byrne can therefore be equated with the concept of 'reasonable reliance'.

Another case highlighting the above is that of *Caparo Industries* where Lord Bridge said that in order for a duty to arise, it was necessary to show that the defendant knew that his statement would be communicated to the plaintiff, either as an individual or as a member of an identifiable class, specifically in connection with a transaction or transactions of a particular kind, and that the plaintiff would be very likely to rely on it in deciding whether or not to enter into a transaction.

Provided that the defendant is aware of the existence of the claimant either as an individual or as a member of an ascertainable class, there is no need that the defendant knows the identity of the claimant. A vital ingredient of the duty is the defendant's knowledge (actual or constructive) of the purpose for which the information is required. In Caparo Industries it was held that, in preparing the audit of the accounts of a public company, the defendants owed no duty either to the plaintiffs either as potential investors or as existing shareholders. The purpose of the audit was to report to the shareholders to enable them to exercise their rights in the management of the company, not to provide information which might assist them in making investment decisions.

In contrast to the position of auditors, surveyors appointed to value a house for mortgage purposes may owe a duty to the purchaser even though the primary purpose of the valuation is to enable the lender to decide whether to advance a loan. This was illustrated in *Harris v Wyre Forest District Council* (1989). This has been justified on the basis that valuers are paid for their services at the mortgagor's expense and understand that a lot of purchasers rely on these reports.

Contributory negligence (disclaimers)

On the assumption that an appropriately worded disclaimer is brought to the claimant's notice, either before or at the time the statement is made, it can be argued that no duty arises because the claimant's reliance would not be reasonable.

However, according to the House of Lords in the case *Smith v Eric S Bush* (1989), the effect of ss.11 (3) and 13 (1) of the Unfair Contract Terms Act 1977 is to subject all exclusion notices which would at common law provide a reasonable defence to an action for negligence, to a test of reasonableness, as provided for in s2 (2) of the act (this only relates to business liability).

Contributory negligence, which is discussed further in the book, is in principle a defence and is available equally to a claim under the Misrepresentation Act 1967.

Third party reliance

There are certain situations in which a duty of care will be imposed on a person (A), who makes a statement to B, as a result that B acts upon it to another's detriment. It is well established, generally, that a solicitor owes no duty of care to third parties. However, this is not always the case. For example, in *White v Jones* (1995), a majority of the House of Lords held the defendant solicitors liable for failing to carry out their clients instructions regarding his will, with the result that the plaintiffs (the intended beneficiaries) lost their legacy.

The duty under White v Jones is not confined to cases relating to wills. In *Gorham v British Telecommunications plc* (CA 2000) an insurance company was held to owe a duty of care to the customer's dependant wife and family where he had intended to create a benefit for them on his death. It was also held in *Spring v Guardian Assurance plc* (HL 1994) that an employer supplying a reference about an employee to a prospective employer owes a duty to the employee to avoid making untrue statements negligently or expressing unfounded opinions, even if held honestly and believed to be true. In this case, it was the opinion of the majority of the Lords that economic loss in the form of failure to obtain employment was clearly foreseeable if a careless reference was given and there was clear proximity of relationship as between employer and employee, so that it was fair, just and reasonable that the law should impose a duty on the employer.

Negligent acts

Although there was originally no liability for pure economic loss caused by acts of negligence, the Hedley Byrne case made major inroads into this area and, although this case was originally confined to misstatements, a trend has developed towards the formulation of a wider principle, applying to both statements and acts.

Damage to third party property

In some cases, damages to property belonging to a third party may prevent the claimant from carrying on their business. In other cases, their contract with the third party may be adversely affected. In neither case can the claimant recover any damages because of a long established rule that no claim will lie in respect of foreseeable economic loss, unaccompanied by physical damage to the property in which the claimant has an interest, either proprietary or possessory.

Defective property

If a claimant has acquired property and discovers it is defective, and money has to be spent on repairing or replacing it, such economic loss can be recovered against a party who has a relevant contractual obligation with the defendant. The claimant cannot bring a claim within the ordinary principles of tort, i.e. those contained within Donoghue v Stevenson, because the claim is concerned with defective goods which can cause personal injury or damage to property rather than the defective product in question.

However, although this was traditionally the case, this fundamental principle was brought into question in the case of *Anns v Merton London Borough Council* (HL 1978). In this case, damages were held to be recoverable by a building owner against a local authority which had negligently inspected and approved defective foundations. In Anns, the decision was justified on the basis that the cause of action arose when the building became an imminent danger to the health and safety of the occupier, who could then recover the cost of averting the potential danger.

Another case which developed this principle was *Junior Books Ltd v Veitchi Co Ltd* (HL 1983). The defendants were held liable for the cost of replacing a defective good supplied by them, even though there was no danger to health and safety. This decision went a considerable way to recognising a general right of recovery for pure economic loss. However, cases following this one have made it very clear that no new principle has been established and each case is viewed on its own merit.

79

Following a number of cases, the whole issue was considered by the Court of Appeal in *Murphy v Brentwood District Council* (HL 1990). The Lords unanimously overruled the findings in Anns so far as it imposed a duty on local authorities, on the ground that where a defect in a building was discovered before any personal injury or damage to property other than the defective house itself had been done, the expense incurred by the building owner in rectifying the defect (including associated costs such as vacating the premises) was pure economic loss and therefore irrecoverable in tort.

There are problems with the decision in Murphy, however. It would seem clear enough that the builder may be liable in accordance with Donoghue v Stevenson principles where a latent defect causes personal injury or damage to another property. In addition, it was thought, by one of the Lords reviewing the case, Lord Bridge, that where a building remained a potential source of injury to persons or property on neighbouring land or on the highway, the owner ought in principle be able to recover in tort from the negligent builder any costs incurred in order to protect himself from potential liabilities to third parties.

Most significantly, the Lords attached weight to the fact that it is the claimant's knowledge of the defect which makes the defect one of quality only, and therefore the loss purely economic. However, such knowledge has not necessarily barred the right of recovery. One such case which highlighted this was *Rimmer v Liverpool City Council* (CA 1984). In this case, the designers and builders of a council flat, the local authority, was liable to a tenant injured by a pane of dangerously thin glass. The tenant knew of the danger and had complained, to no avail. It was considered that it was not practical for the tenant to either leave the flat or to change the pane of glass himself, although damages were reduced for contributory negligence.

Psychiatric illness

In *Alcock v Chief Constable of South Yorkshire* (HL 1991) Lord Ackner stated that shock "involves the sudden appreciation by sight or sound of a horrifying event, which violently agitates the mind".

Shock must manifest itself in some recognisable psychiatric or physical illness. Mere grief or emotional upset is not actionable, although mental distress suffered as a result of negligently inflicted injuries may be taken into account in the assessment of damages for pain and suffering.

Shock victims fall into two (very) broad groups, those who are unwilling participants in the events causing shock (known as primary victims) and those who are merely passive and unwilling victims (secondary victims). In relation to the first group, Lord Ackner said that if the defendants negligent conduct foreseeably puts the plaintiff in that position it follows that there will be a sufficiently proximate relationship between them, though if personal injury of some kind to the plaintiff is reasonably foreseeable as the result of an accident the defendant is liable for psychiatric injury (even though no physical injury occurs) and the plaintiff need not prove that injury by shock was foreseeable because the defendant must take his victim as he finds him.

Subsequent cases have established three types of primary victim, namely those who are put in reasonable fear for their own safety, rescuers and those who reasonably believe that they are about to be, or have been, the involuntary cause of another's death or injury. Such persons will recover if shock to them was reasonably foreseeable or if personal injury of some kind was foreseeable.

Where shock victims fall within the second category of groups a more complex analysis is required. It was held in Alcock that in order to recover damages, the plaintiff had to prove the following:

81

- that his relationship to the primary victim was sufficiently close that it was reasonably foreseeable that he might suffer shock if he apprehended that the victim had been, or might be, injured;
- that he was temporally and spatially close to the scene of the accident or its immediate aftermath;
- that he suffered shock through sight or hearing of the accident or its immediate aftermath.

One matter not covered in Alcock was whether a plaintiff could recover for shock caused as a result of witnessing the destruction of property. In *Attia v British Gas plc* (CA 1988) it was held that there was no principle of law that shock in such circumstances could never be regarded as foreseeable. However, since the defendants in that case admitted to owing a duty in respect of the damage to the plaintiff's home, the shock issue was treated as one of remoteness rather than duty.

Omissions

In tort, as a general rule, the defendant does not owe a duty to take positive action to prevent harm to others. For example, the failure of a public authority to exercise a statutory power, or a statutory duty, will not normally give rise to a common law duty (see *Stovin v Wise* HL 1996). The mere existence of statutory powers and duties did not create a parallel common law duty.

This was highlighted in the case of *Gorringe v Calderdale* (2004) where the highway authorities failure to paint a marking or to erect a road sign warning of a dangerous stretch of road did not give rise to a duty of care to the claimant.

Negligence-breach of duty

Once it has been established that a duty of care is owed to a claimant, it must then be proven that the defendant was in breach of that duty.

The key definition of negligence and duty of care was defined in *Blythe v Birmingham Waterworks* Co (1856). In this case, a wooden plug in a water main became loose in a severe frost. The plug led to a pipe which in turn went up the street. However, this pipe was blocked with ice, and the water instead flooded the claimant's house. The claimant sued in negligence. In this case, Alderson B defined negligence as:

"the omission to do something which a reasonable man, guided upon those considerations which ordinarily regulate the conduct of human affairs, would do, or doing something which a prudent and reasonable man would not do".

The key word here is *"reasonable man"*. The standard of care required of the defendant is that of the hypothetical reasonable man. This standard is objective as it does not take into account particular traits of an individual. In *Hall v Brooklands Auto Racing Club* (1933) Greer LJ described such a person as:

- the 'man in the street'; or
- 'the man on the Clapham Omnibus; or
- 'the man who takes the magazines at home, and in the evening pushes the lawnmower in his shirt sleeves'

The reasonable person is therefore an 'average' person and not perfect.

The standard of reasonable care is invariable in the sense that the law does not recognise differing degrees of negligence but it is an infinitely flexible concept enabling the court in any given situation to impose standards ranging from high to low.

What is reasonable conduct varies with the particular circumstance, and liability depends ultimately what the reasonable man would have foreseen, which in turn may depend upon what particular knowledge and experience, if any, is to be attributed to him. However, although a defendant is not negligent if the consequences of his conduct were unforeseeable, it does not necessarily follow that the defendant will be responsible for all foreseeable consequences. In practice the courts evaluate a defendant's behaviour in terms of risk, so that he will be seen to be negligent if the claimant is exposed to an unreasonable risk of harm.

Special standards of care

There are certain situations in which the courts will apply a different standard of care from that of the 'reasonable' person:
- Where the defendant has a particular skill
- Where the defendant has a particular lack of skill
- Where the defendant is a child
- Where the defendant is competing in or watching a sporting event.

Skilled or professional defendants

The standard of care applied to professional with a particular skill or expertise is that of the reasonable person with the same skill or expertise. For example a doctor would be expected to show a greater degree of skill and care to a patient than 'the man on the Clapham omnibus'. See below.

Magnitude of the risk

The degree of care which the law expects must be commensurate with the risk created. Two factors are involved, namely the likelihood that harm will be caused and the potential gravity of that harm. In the case *Bolton v Stone* (HL 1951) the plaintiff was standing in the road when she was struck by a cricket ball which had been hit out of the defendants ground. There was some evidence that this had happened before on an infrequent basis, i.e. six times in thirty years, so that the risk was one of which the defendants were aware and which was reasonably foreseeable. However, the defendants were not held liable because the risk was so small that they were perfectly justified in not taking any further measures to eliminate that risk.

Another case illustrating magnitude and gravity of the risk is that of *Paris v Stepney B.C* (HL 1951) where a person with one eye, a garage worker, became totally blind after being struck in the eye by a metal chip which flew from a bolt which he was trying to hammer loose. The defendants, his employers, were held liable for failing to provide him with safety goggles, even though they were justified in not providing such equipment to a person with normal sight. Although the risk was small, the injury to this particular person was very serious.

Another case which illustrates the magnitude of risk is that of *Watson v British Boxing Board of Control* (2001) where the board breached its duty in failing to inform itself adequately about the risks inherent to a blow to the head and by failing to provide resuscitation equipment to be provided at the ringside together with persons able to operate it. The degree of risk to which a claimant is exposed will also depend upon any physical abnormality from which he may suffer so that, if such abnormality is or ought to be known to the defendant, that is a factor which should be taken into account.

Characteristics of the defendant

The general legal standard does not take into account the personal characteristics of a particular defendant. Inexperience, lack of intelligence or other provide no defence to negligence. For example, a partially sighted driver owes the same level of duty as a normally sighted driver. However, two types of defendant require mention.

Evidence of negligence

It is for the claimant to prove, on a balance of probabilities, that the defendant was negligent. This is subject to the proviso contained within the Civil Evidence Act 1968 s.11, that proof that a person stands convicted of an offence is conclusive evidence in civil proceedings that he did commit it unless the contrary is proved. The effect of this provision is to shift the burden of proof where the claimant proves that the defendant has been convicted of an offence involving conduct complained of as negligent, such as careless driving.

In order to discharge the burden of proof the claimant must usually prove particular conduct on the part of the defendant which can be regarded as negligent. The claimant will not be able to do so, however, if he does not know how the accident was caused and, in such a case, the maxim *res ipsa loquitur* (the thing speaks for itself) may be relied on. This is a rule of evidence that the claimant, who is unable to explain how the accident happened, asks the court to make a *prima facie* finding of negligence, which it is then for the defendant to rebut if he or she can. There are three conditions necessary for the application of the doctrine which arose out of *Scott v London and St Katherines Docks Co (EC 1865):* there must be an absence of an explanation as to how the accident happened, the 'thing' which causes the damage must be under control of the defendant (or someone for whose negligence he is responsible) and the accident must be such as would not ordinarily occur without negligence.

****

2.2

Negligence-Causation and Remoteness of Damage

Causation

It must first be established that the breach was the cause of the damage, or materially contributed to the damage. In determining this issue, it is usual to employ the 'but for' test, the function of which is to eliminate those factors which could not have had any causal effect. One case which illustrates this is *Cork v Kirby Maclean 1952* Where a workman, an epileptic, was set to work painting the roof inside a factory, which necessitated his doing the work from a platform some 23 feet above the floor of the factory. The platform was some 27 inches wide and was used for the deposit of the workman's brush and bucket. There were no guard-rails or toe boards. The workman fell from the platform and was killed. In this case, Lord Denning stated:

...if the damage would not have happened but for a particular fault, then that fault is the cause of the damage; if it would have happened just the same, fault or no fault, the fault is not the cause of the damage.

Another case is *Barnett v Chelsea and Kensington Hospital Management Committee* (HC 1969) where the failure of a casualty officer to examine a patient, who subsequently died of arsenic poisoning, was held not to have been a cause of death because evidence showed that the patient would have probably died in any event.

Difficulties may arise where the precise cause of the damage is unknown. In *McGhee v National Coal Board* (HL 1972) the patient contracted dermatitis as a result of exposure to abrasive dust at work. His employers were not at fault for the exposure during the normal course of his work, but were found to be negligent for failing to provide washing facilities with the result that he was caked in dust for longer than necessary as he cycled home. The plaintiff succeeded on the ground that it was sufficient to show that the defendant's breach materially increased the risk of injury, even though medical knowledge at the time was unable to establish the breach as the probable cause. This decision had far reaching effects, particularly in cases of medical negligence.

An attempt was made in *Hotson v East Berkshire Area Health Authority* (HL 1987) to extend the principle so as to impose a liability in respect of the loss of a chance of recovery. In this case, the plaintiff injured his hip in a fall and, as a result of negligent medical diagnosis, suffered a permanent deformity the risk of which would have been reduced by 25 per cent had the proper treatment been given at the time. The Court of Appeal upheld the finding but this was overturned by the House of Lords on the grounds that there was no principle in law which would have justified a discount from the full measure of damages.

In cases where successive acts cause damage, the position is more complex. In *Baker v Willoughby* (HL 1970) the plaintiff's leg was injured through the defendant's negligence, and some time later, before the trial, he was shot in the same leg during a robbery. The leg was then amputated. It was held in this case that the plaintiff's right of recovery was not limited to the loss suffered only before the date of the robbery, but that he was entitled to damages that he would have received had there been no subsequent injury.

In another case, *Jobling v Associated Dairies Limited* (HL 1980) the defendant's negligence caused a reduction in the plaintiffs earning capacity. Three years later, but before the trial, the defendant was found to be suffering from another complaint, wholly unrelated to the original accident, which totally incapacitated him. The defendant's were held liable only for the loss up to the time of the plaintiff's disablement.

Remoteness of damage

The plaintiff is not entitled to compensation for every consequence of the defendant's wrong. In order to contain the defendant's liability within reasonable bounds, a line is drawn, and the consequences that fall on the far side of the line are said to be too remote and not having been caused in law by the defendant's breach of duty.

There are a number of cases which have provided tests of remoteness of damage. In *Re Polemis and Furness, Withy and Co* (CA 1921) a ship's cargo of benzene had leaked filling the hold with inflammable vapour. Stevedores unloading the vessel negligently dropped a plank in the hold, and the defendant employers were held liable for the destruction of the ship in the blaze that followed because that loss was a direct, although unforeseeable consequence of the negligence.

Whilst not denying the relevance of foreseeability to the existence of a duty, the case did decide that it was not relevant in determining for what consequences the defendant should pay.

However, in another case, *Overseas Tankship (UK) Ltd v Morts Dock Engineering Co Ltd (The Wagon Mound)*, 1961 this approach was disproved. A test of reasonable foresight of consequence was substituted for that of directness. The defendants, in this case, negligently discharged into Sydney Harbour a large quantity of fuel oil which drifted to the plaintiff's wharf whilst welding was in progress. The plaintiff's discontinued their operations, but later resumed following an assurance that there was no danger of the oil igniting. A fire did eventually break out, causing damage to the wharf and to two ships upon which work was being carried out. It was found as a fact that some damage to the wharf was reasonably foreseeable by way of fouling the slipway, but that, in view of expert evidence, it was unforeseeable that the oil would ignite. The defendant's were, accordingly, held not liable.

Manner of occurrence

In *Hughes v Lord Advocate* (HL 1963) post office employees negligently left a manhole uncovered with a canvas shelter over it, surrounded by paraffin lamps. The plaintiff, aged eight, took none of the lamps into the shelter and knocked it into the manhole. There was an explosion, following an unusual combination of circumstances, in which the boy was badly burned. Although the explosion was unforeseeable, the defendants were held liable because burns from the lamp were foreseeable, and it was immaterial that the precise chain of events leading to the injury was not.

A contrasting case is that of *Doughty v Turner Manufacturing Co Ltd* (CA 1964) in which the defendant's employee dropped an asbestos cover into a vat of molten liquid which, due to an unforeseeable chemical reaction, erupted and burned a fellow worker standing nearby. It was held that, even if injury by splashing were foreseeable the eruption was not, and the plaintiff failed. This case is at odds with Hughes (above) because if it accepted that some injury by burning was foreseeable, then it ought not to matter that the way in which it occurred was not.

Type of damage

The exact nature of the damage need not be foreseeable, provided it is of a type that could have been foreseen. The difficulty here, of defining damage 'of a type' is illustrated by two contrasting cases. The first case, *Bradford v Robinson Rentals Ltd* (HC 1967) a van driver sent on a long journey in an unheated vehicle in severe weather was able to recover damages for frostbite because, although not in itself foreseeable, it was in the broad class of foreseeable risk arising from exposure to severe cold.

The second case, *Tremain v Pike* (HC 1969) the defendant's alleged negligence caused his farm to become rat-infested with the result that the plaintiff contracted a rare disease by contact with rats urine. It was held that, even if negligence had been proved, the plaintiff could not succeed because although injury from rat bites or food contamination was foreseeable, this particularly rare disease was entirely different in kind.

Extent of damage

When considering the extent of damage, it doesn't matter that the actual damage is far greater in extent than could have been foreseen. In *Vacwell Engineering Co Ltd v B.D.H. Chemicals Ltd* (CA 1971) the plaintiffs purchased a chemical manufactured and supplied by the defendants, who failed to give warning that it was liable to cause a minor explosion on contact with water. The plaintiff's employee placed a large amount of the chemical in a sink and an explosion of unforeseeable violence badly damaged the premises. Since the explosion and subsequent damage were foreseeable, even though the extent was not, the defendants were held liable.

A similar rule operates where the claimant suffers foreseeable personal injury which is exacerbated by some pre-existing physical or psychic abnormality. This so called "egg-shell skull" principle imposes liability on the defendant for harm which is not only greater in extent than, but which is of an entirely different kind to, that which is foreseeable. In *Smith v Leech Brain and Co Ltd* (HC 1962) a workman who had a predisposition to cancer received a burn on the lip from molten metal due to a colleague's negligence. The defendants were held liable for his subsequent death from cancer triggered by the burn.

The principle applies equally to a claimant who suffers from nervous shock. In *Meah v McCreamer* (HC 1985) the plaintiff underwent a marked personality change brought about by injuries received in a collision for which the defendant was responsible. This led him to commit a series of assaults for which he received a life sentence. He recovered damages for loss of liberty.

Intervening causes

In some cases, the claimant's damage is alleged to be attributable not to the defendant's breach of duty, but to some intervening event which breaks the chain of causation. Such an event is called a *novus actus interveniens* and is usually dealt with as part of the issue of remoteness because even though the damage would not have occurred "but for" the defendants breach, it may still be regarded in law as falling outside the scope of the risk created by the original fault. One such case that illustrates this is *McKew v Holland* and *Hannen and Cubitts* (Scotland) Ltd (HL 1969) where the plaintiff's leg occasionally gave way without warning as a result of the defendant's negligence. On one such occasion he fractured his ankle as a result of descending a flight of stairs where his leg gave way.

The defendant's were held not liable for this further injury because, although foreseeable, the plaintiff's conduct was *so* unreasonable as to amount to a *novus actus*. However, each case on its own merit.

Whether the issue is seen as *novus actus* or of contributory negligence (which is the more common approach) will depend upon the nature of the plaintiff's conduct and it may be that a positive act is more likely to break the causal chain than a mere omission.

Intervention of a third party

According to Lord Reid in *Dorset Yacht Co Ltd v Home Office* (HL 1970) the intervention of a third party must have been something very likely to happen if it is not regarded as breaking the chain of causation. The question is what is the potential liability of a defendant for the criminal act of another? In the case *Knightly v Johns* (CA 1982) the defendant negligently caused a crash on a dangerous bend in a one-way tunnel. The police inspector at the scene of the accident forgot to close the tunnel to oncoming traffic as he ought to have done in accordance with standing orders, so he ordered the plaintiff officer to ride back on his motorcycle against the flow of traffic in order to do so, and the plaintiff was injured in a further collision. It was said that, in considering whether the intervening act of a third party breaks the chain of causation, the test is whether the damage is reasonably foreseeable in the sense of being a 'natural and probable' result of the defendant's breach. A deliberate decision to do a positive act is more likely to break the chain than a mere omission. In this case, the inspector's errors amounted to tortuous negligence which cannot be described as the natural and probable consequence of the original collision, and the defendant was held not liable.

Intervening natural force

The defendant will not normally be held liable for damage suffered as the immediate consequence of a natural event which occurs independently of the breach. In the case *Carslogie Steamship Co Ltd v Royal Norwegian Government* (HL 1952) the defendants were held not liable for storm damage suffered by a ship during a voyage to a place where repairs to collision damage caused by the defendant's negligence were to be done, even though that voyage would not have been undertaken had the collision not occurred.

Contributory Negligence

Since the passage of the Law Reform (Contributory Negligence) Act 1945 contributory negligence is no longer a complete bar to recovery but, in accordance with s.1(1) of the act, will result in a reduction of damages to such an extent as is seen as just and equitable.

The Act applies where the damage is attributable to the fault of both parties, and 'fault' is defined in section 4 to mean "negligence, breach of statutory duty, or other act or omission which gives rise to a liability in tort or would, apart from this act, give rise to the defence of contributory negligence". The defence, therefore, applies to actions other than negligence, though it does not apply to deceit or intentional interference with goods - Torts (Interference With Goods) Act 1977 s.11).

Causation

The damage suffered must be caused partly by the fault of the claimant and it is therefore irrelevant that the claimant's fault was nothing to do with the accident. Thus, reductions in damages have been made for failure to wear a seat belt or a crash helmet and for travelling in a vehicle with a drunk driver.

One case which highlights this is *Jones v Livox Quarries Ltd (CA 1952)*. The plaintiff, contrary to instructions, stood on a rear towbar of a vehicle and was injured when another vehicle ran into the back of it. In this case, damages were reduced as the claimant had exposed himself to risk. The claimant is expected to show an objective standard of care in much the same way as the defendant must to avoid tortuous negligence. There are particular cases in contributory negligence, children, old or infirm persons and rescuers merit special attention.

Children

As a matter of law thee is no age below which it can be said that a child is incapable of contributory negligence. However, the degree of care expected must be apportioned to the age of the child. For example, in *Gough v Thorne (CA 1966)* a 13 year old girl who was knocked down by a negligent motorist when she stepped past a stationary lorry whose driver had beckoned her to cross, was held not guilty of contributory negligence. However, in *Morales v Eccleston* (CA 1991) an 11 year old boy who was struck by the defendant driver while kicking a ball in the middle of the road with traffic passing in either direction had his damages reduced by 75 per cent.

Old or infirm persons

When assessing whether such a person is guilty of contributory negligence, the age and infirmity and its impact on the alleged negligence is taken into account.

Rescuers

It is not very often, for obvious reasons, that a rescuer will be found guilty of contributory negligence. In *Brandon v Osborne, Garret and Co Ltd* (HC 1924) the defendants negligently allowed a sheet of glass to fall from their shop roof and the plaintiff, believing her husband to be in danger, tried to pull him away and injured her leg. She was held to not be contributorily negligent. A similar principle applies where the claimant is injured in trying to extricate himself or herself from a perilous situation in which the defendants negligence has placed them, even though, with hindsight the claimant is shown to have chosen the wrong course of action. As with all such cases, each case is viewed on its own merit.

Apportionment

Apportionment is on a just and equitable basis according to the 1945 Act and, in assessing the claimant's reduction, the court may take into account both the potency of his act and the degree of blameworthiness to be attached to it. The Court of Appeal has held, in *Johnson v Tennant Bros Ltd* (CA 1954) that no apportionment should be made unless one of the parties is at least 10 per cent to blame. However, the decisions concerning apportionment is left, mainly, to judicial discretion.

Violenti Non Fit Injuria

This maxim embodies a principle that a person who expressly or impliedly agrees with another to run the risk of harm created by that other person cannot then sue in respect of damage suffered as a result of the materialisation of that risk. The defence is called consent or voluntary assumption of risk and, if successful, is a complete bar to recovery.

For the defence to apply the defendant must have committed what would, in the absence of any consent, amount to a tort. The defendant must prove not only that the claimant consented to the risk of actual damage, but also that he or she agreed to waive their right of action in respect of that damage.

Knowledge of the risk

Knowledge of the risk does not amount to consent. It must be found that the claimant, with full knowledge of the risk, agreed to incur it.

Agreement

In relation to agreement, in addition to the claimant being willing to take the risk, there must be evidence that the claimant has expressly or impliedly agreed to waive his or her course of action. An express antecedent agreement to relieve the defendant of liability for future negligence operates in effect as an exclusion notice and is therefore subject to the Unfair Contract terms Act 1977. Section 2(1) renders void any purported exclusion of liability for death or personal injury caused by negligence and, in the case of other loss or damage, s.2(2) subjects such an exclusion to a test of reasonableness. Section 2(3) further provides that a persons agreement to, or awareness of, such a notice is not of itself to be taken as indicating his voluntary acceptance of any risk. These provisions only apply to business liability.

In some circumstances the conduct of the parties may enable an inference to be drawn that the claimant has impliedly agreed to waive his legal rights in respect of future negligence. One such case was *Morris v Murray* (CA 1990). The defence applied when, in poor weather conditions, the defendant, who to the plaintiff's knowledge was extremely drunk, took the plaintiff for a spin and crashed the aircraft immediately after takeoff.

With negligence cases in the sporting arena, the potential liability of the participant depends upon the standard of care owed. In any sporting event, the spectator may be taken to have accepted the risks incidental to the game, for example, being hit by a cricket ball whilst watching a game of cricket. In the case *Wooldridge v Sumner* (CA 1963) it was stated that sportsmen and women have a duty not to behave with reckless disregard for the spectator. This applies to the duty of care required between one player and another. In *Watson v British Boxing Board of Control* (2001) it was pointed out that where the plaintiff consents to injury by an opponent in a boxing ring he does not consent to injury resulting from inadequate safety arrangements by the sports governing body after being hit.

Ex Turpi Causa

Where an alleged wrong occurs whilst the claimant is engaged in criminal activity, the claim may be barred because ex *turpi causa non oritur actio (no action can be founded on an illegal act).* This principle is based on public policy and may also apply where the claimant's conduct is immoral. The difficulty is deciding which types of conduct are considered sufficiently heinous for the purposes of defence. Some cases have found that it will apply where it would be impossible to determine an appropriate standard of care, whilst others have suggested that the claimant ought not to succeed if to permit him to do so would be an affront to the public conscience.

In *Clunis v Camden and Islington Health Authority* (CA 1998) the plaintiff, who had a long history of mental illness, was convicted of manslaughter and ordered to be detained in a secure hospital. He sued the defendant for negligence for failing to take reasonable care to provide him with after care services following his discharge from hospital where he had been detained under the Mental Health Act 1983.

It was held that, despite a successful plea of diminished responsibility at the criminal trial, his action was barred on the grounds of public policy since he was directly implicated in the illegality and must be taken to have known that what he was doing was wrong.

In *Vellino v Chief Constable of Greater Manchester Police* (CA 2001) the claimant suffered brain damage when he attempted to escape from police custody by jumping though a window on the second floor. Negligence was claimed on the part of the arresting officers, alleging that they had stood by and let him jump. The Court of Appeal held that the claim was untenable because the defendant had to rely on his own criminal conduct in escaping lawful custody to found his claim.

****

2.3

Negligence-Employers Liability

In addition to common law duty, there is a large body of statutory obligations which the employer has to abide by when protecting its workforce. In relation to accidents and other forms of negligence it is common for employers to sue both in negligence and breach of statutory duty. Employers have a statutory duty to insure against liability, as laid down by the Employers Liability (Compulsory Insurance) Act 1969.

Nature of the duty

Although there once existed the doctrine of common employment, in which there was an implied term in a contract of employment that employees accepted risks incidental to their employment, the law has changed significantly.

The doctrine of common employment was abolished in 1948 and, as the law has evolved, employers have a personal duty and a vicarious liability towards their employees. Traditionally, the duty is said to be threefold, which was highlighted in the case of *Wilsons and Clyde Coal Co Ltd v English* (HL 1938), namely "the provision of a competent staff of men, adequate material and a proper system and effective supervision". The duty is not absolute but is discharged by the exercise of reasonable care and is thus similar to the duty of care in the tort of negligence generally. Although most of the cases concern work accidents, the duty extends to guarding against disease and gradual deterioration in health as a result of adverse working conditions. This was illustrated in the case of *Thompson v Smith's Ship repairers (North Shields) Ltd* (HC 1984). However, it does not extend to the prevention of economic loss by, for example, advising the employee to take out insurance nor the prevention of injury to health caused by self-induced intoxication.

Safe plant and equipment

The employer has a duty to take reasonable care to provide proper plant and equipment and to maintain them so as to keep them in good order. This includes the provision of protective devices and clothing appropriate to the job, and also a warning or exhortation from the employer to make use of such equipment.

One case which highlights this is *Bux v Slough Metals Ltd* (CA 1973) where the plaintiff, a foundry worker, lost the sight of one eye when splashed with molten metal. Although the employer had, in compliance with statutory regulations, provided protective goggles, he was held liable for breach of his common law duty, which extended to persuading and even insisting on the use of protective equipment. Most employees will now be protected by the Personal Protective Equipment at Work Regulations 1992, which impose a statutory duty to take all reasonable steps to see that protective equipment is properly used, though it is the employee's duty to use it.

In relation to injury caused by defective equipment, in the case *Davie v New Merton Board Mills Ltd* (HL 1959) it was held that the duty to provide proper tools was satisfied by purchase from a reputable supplier. This decision has now been reversed however, by the Employer's Liability (Defective Equipment) Act 1969, which renders an employer personally liable in negligence if two conditions are met: first, that the employee is injured in the course of his employment by a defect in equipment issued by the employer for the purposes of the employer's business and, secondly, that the defect is attributable wholly or partly to the fault of a third party, (whether identifiable or not. Such a third party could be the manufacturer. Strict liability is thus imposed upon the employer if his employee can prove that some third party was at fault, though contributory negligence can be used as a defence by that third party.

The employee might also be able to rely on the Provision and Use of Work Equipment Regulations 1992 which provide that employers must ensure that work equipment is so constructed or adapted as to be suitable for the purpose for which it is to be used or provided, and that such equipment is maintained in an efficient state.

Safe system of work

A safe system of work means the organisation of work, the manner in which it is to be carried out, the organising and planning of numbers of men and women and their tasks and the instructions given to these workers. One case illustrating this is *Johnstone v Bloomsbury Health Authority* (CA 1991) where it was held that requiring the plaintiff to work such long hours as might foreseeably injure his health could constitute a breach of duty. In *Walker v Nortumberland County Council* (HC 1995) the plaintiff suffered a nervous breakdown as a result of the employers broken promise to provide a safe system of work to reduce his workload. Very little was actually provided and he suffered a second breakdown which forced him to stop work permanently. His employers were held liable for failing to provide a safe place of work in that they continued to employ him without adequate assistance. In *Waters v Commissioner of Police of the Metropolis* (2000) the House of Lords held that an employer is under a duty to take reasonable care to protect its employees from harm, including workplace bullying and psychiatric harm, where the employer knows or can foresee that an employee might suffer this harm through the acts of fellow employees.

In *Hatton v Sutherland* (2002) the Court of Appeal ruled that claims for stress induced psychiatric illness follow the standard principles governing personal injury claims in that no special control mechanisms are applied to claims for psychiatric or physical injury arising from stress at work. The ordinary principles of employer's liability apply and the questions to be determined are:

- was there a breach of employer's duty of care which caused psychiatric harm to the employee?
- Was the psychiatric harm to that particular employee reasonably foreseeable?

The duty of care does not arise where the employer is unaware of the employee's vulnerability to stress induced illness or of an imminent psychiatric breakdown.

Safe premises

The employer's obligation includes making the premises as safe as possible. However, the employer is not required to eliminate every foreseeable risk if the burden in so doing is too onerous. In *Wilson v Tyneside Window Cleaning* (CA 1958) where it was held that the duty exists equally in relation to premises in the occupation or control of the third party. In appropriate circumstances an employer must be expected to go and inspect the premises to see that they are reasonably safe for the work to be carried out on them. However, the fact that the employer does not have control of the workplace is important in determining whether he has been negligent. Most workplaces are now governed by the Workplace (Health, Safety and Welfare) Regulations 1992.

Scope of the duty

The scope of the duty relates to the employer-employee and does not extend to an independent contractor. The duty is personal and non-delegable, so that the employer does not discharge his duty by entrusting its performance to another, whether that be an employer or independent contractor.

VICARIOUS LIABILITY

The employer-employee relationship is the most common example of vicarious liability. The negligence committed by an employee can thus ultimately be the liability of the employer.

OCCUPIERS LIABILITY

The occupier of a property in respect of loss or injury suffered by those who enter a property or its grounds lawfully is governed by the Occupiers Liability Act 1957. prior to this Act, the extent of liability owed by an occupier depended upon the relationship with the person injured. The OLA 1957 abolished this in favour of two categories:

- Lawful visitors, who were protected by the Act
- All others who were not protected

This Act was supplemented by the Occupiers Liability Act 1984 which covers injuries to trespassers. Section 2(1) of the 1957 Act provides:

"An occupier owes the same duty, the 'common duty of care' to all his visitors, except in so far as he is free to, and does extend, restrict, modify or exclude his duty to any visitor or visitors by agreement or otherwise".

Who is an occupier?

The Act contains no clear definition of an "occupier". This is simply a term to denote a person who has a sufficient degree of control over premises to put him under a duty of care towards those who lawfully come on to the premises. Control is the decisive factor and it is not material that the occupier has no interest in the land, he could be tenant, lessee, licensee or any other person having the right to possession. One case illustrating this is *AMF International Ltd v Magnet Bowling Ltd* (HC 1968) where building contractors were held to be joint occupiers along with the building owners. A landlord who has let his property to a tenant will not be the occupier of the demised parts but will still be held to be the occupier of those parts, i.e. common parts, not demised to the tenant.

The premises

The definition of premises is wide and covers not only land and buildings. By s.1 (3)(a) of the Act, the statutory provisions extend to any fixed or moveable structure, including any vessel, vehicle or aircraft. This is apt to include not only structures of a permanent nature but also temporary structures such as ladders and scaffolding.

Visitors

The statutory duty is owed only to visitors who, by s.1 (2) are those who would, at common law, have been either invitees or licensees. For a licence to have been inferred there must be evidence that the occupier has permitted entry as opposed to merely tolerating it, as there is no positive obligation to keep the trespasser out. Repeated trespass of itself confers no licence. However, in some cases the courts have gone to great lengths to infer the existence of a licence. One case illustrating this is *Lowery v Walker* (HL 1911) where members of the public had for many years used the defendant's field as a short cut to the railway station. The defendant had often prevented them from so doing but did nothing further to stop them until, without warning, he turned a savage horse loose in the field. The animal attacked and injured the plaintiff who then sued and succeeded in his action on the basis that he was a licensee not a trespasser.

There are a number of other types of entrant that must be considered. Those who enter premises for any purpose in the exercise of a right conferred by law are treated, by s.2(6) of the Act as having the occupiers permission to be there for that purpose (whether they have it or not). Secondly, s.5(1) provides that where a person enters under the terms of a contract with the occupier there is, in the absence of express provision in the contract, an implied term that the entrant is owed the common duty of care and, according to *Sole v W.J Hallt Ltd* (HC 1973) he may frame his claim either in contract or under the 1957 Act. It is further provided by s.3(1) that where a person contracts with the occupier on the basis that a third party is to have access to the premises, the duty owed by the occupier to such third party as his visitor cannot be reduced by the terms of the contract to a level lower than the common duty of care. Conversely, if the contract imposes upon the occupier any obligation which exceeds the requirements of the statutory duty, then the third party is entitled to the benefit of that additional obligation. Thirdly, those who use public or private rights of way are not visitors for the purposes of the 1957 Act, though the user of a private right of way is now owed a duty under the Occupiers Liability Act 1984 (see later).

Exclusions

As has been outlined, the duty owed to a contractual entrant is governed by the terms of the contract and a person who enters under a contract to which he is not party is, at the very least, owed a duty of care. In the case of no-contractual entrants, it is clear that, at common law, an occupier may be able to exclude or limit his liability by notice, provided that reasonable steps are taken to bring it to the visitor's attention and that the notice is clear and not misleading in any way. One case that illustrates this is *Ashdown v Samuel Williams and Sons* (CA 1956) where it was held that the plaintiff, who was injured by the negligent shunting of a railway wagon upon the defendants premises, was defeated in her claim by exclusion notices erected by the defendant saying that person entered at their own risk and no liability would be accepted for loss or damage, whether caused by negligence or otherwise.

The basic principle is that if an occupier can prevent people from entering his premises, then he can equally impose conditions, subject to which entry is permitted. However, the power of the occupier to exclude or restrict his liability for death or injury has been severely reduced by s.2 of the Unfair Contract Terms Act 1977. This section provides that a person cannot, by reference to a contract term or to a notice, exclude or restrict his liability for death or personal injury caused by negligence unless the term or contents of the notice satisfies the requirement of reasonableness.

The operations of s.2 of the Act is confined to those situations where there is business liability which is defined in s.1(3) as liability for breach of duty arising from things done in the course of a business or from the occupation of premises used for the business purposes of the occupier.

Common duty of care
The common duty of care is defined in s.2 (2) as:

"a duty to take such care as in all circumstances is reasonable to see that the visitor will be reasonably safe in using the premises for the purposes for which he is invited or permitted to be there"

This is similar to the common duty of care and may extend to taking steps to see that a visitor does not deliberately harm other visitors by foreseeably likely conduct. Whether the occupier has charged it depends on the facts, taking into account such matters as the nature of the danger, the purpose of the visit and the knowledge of the parties. In particular, there is provision in the act for Children, those with special skills, warning notices and independent contractors.

Children
The Act provides that the amount of care which an occupier can expect from a visitor will depend on certain factors. By s.2(3)(a) the occupier must be prepared for children to be less careful than an adult. However, case law has sought to balance responsibility between occupiers and parents.

The level of care expected will depend on the nature of the risk and the age and awareness of the child. For example, in the case *Titchener v BRB* 1983 no duty was owed to a 15 year old boy who was struck by a train whilst walking on a railway line at night as he was aware of the dangers posed by his activity.

Special skills
Section 2(3)(b) provides that:

"an occupier may expect that a person, in the exercise of his calling, will appreciate and guard against any special risks ordinarily incident to it, so far as the occupier leaves him free to do so".

In the case *Roles v Nathan* (CA 1963) the defendant was held not liable for the death of two chimney sweeps killed by carbon monoxide fumes while sealing up a flue in the defendant's boiler. If the same people had fallen through the floor because of a rotten floorboard the position would have been different.

Warnings

The occupier may, in accordance with s.2(4)(a) of the Act, discharge his duty by warning his visitor of the particular danger, provided that the notice is effective and the warning is sufficient to ensure that the visitor is reasonably safe. Warning notices have to be distinguished from exclusion notices. By sufficient warning the occupier discharges his duty, whereas exclusion purports to take away the right of recovery in respect of a breach. To be effective a warning must sufficiently identify the source of the danger.

Independent contractors

Where a visitor suffers damage due to faulty construction, maintenance or repair work by an independent contractor employed by the occupier, s 2 (4)(b) provides that the occupier will not be liable if it was reasonable to entrust the work to a contractor and he took such steps as he reasonably ought to see that the contractor was competent and had done the work properly. The occupier is not necessarily expected to check work of a technical nature although in the case of a complex project he may be under a duty to have the contractor's work supervised by a qualified specialist such as an architect or surveyor.

Defences
The provisions of the Law Reform (Contributory Negligence) Act 1945 apply and s.2(5) of the 1957 Act provides that an occupier is not liable in respect of risks which the visitor willingly accepts, thus allowing for the defence of *volenti non fit inujuria*. However, where there is business liability within the meaning of the Unfair Contract Terms Act 1977, s.2(3) of that Act provides that a person's agreement to or awareness of a notice purporting to exclude liability for negligence is not of itself to be taken as indicating his voluntary acceptance of the risk.

The Occupiers Liability Act 1984
The 1984 OLA extended the protection of the law to cover:

Trespassers
People lawfully exercising rights of way
Visitors to land covered by section 60 of the National Parks and Access to the Countryside Act 1949 and 'right to room' legislation.

The 1984 Occupiers Liability Act governs the liability of an occupier to "persons other than his visitors" in respect of injury suffered by them on the premises due to the state of the premises or to things done or needing to be done to them. The term "persons other than his visitors" includes trespassers and persons exercising private rights of way, but those using public rights of way.

The scope of the duty
Section 1(3) of the 1984 Act provides that the occupier owes a duty if:
-   he is aware of the danger or has reasonable grounds to believe that it exists;

- he knows or has reasonable grounds to believe that the non visitor is in the vicinity of the danger concerned or that he may come into the vicinity of the danger; and
- the risk is one against which, in all the circumstances of the case, he may be reasonably expected to offer the non-visitor some protection.

Whilst paragraph (c) clearly adopts an objective test, paragraphs (a) and (b) import a subjective element in that the existence of a duty depends upon the occupiers actual knowledge of facts which should lead him to conclude that a danger exists. If the occupier is not aware of these facts he may not owe a duty.

In the case *Rhind v Astbury* (2004) the claimant accepted that he was a trespasser when he dived into shallow water to retrieve a football, but he argued that his injury was caused by a fibreglass container on the bed of the lake which constituted a danger within the meaning of s.1 (3) of the 1984 Act. The Court of Appeal held that the claimant had failed to establish a duty of care under s.1(3) since the defendant was unaware of the existence of the container and had no reasonable grounds for suspecting that the danger existed.

It is to be noted that the statutory duty applies only to personal injury or death. Liability for loss of, or damage to, property is expressly excluded by s. 1(8).

Defences
Section 1(5) of the Act provides that the occupier may, in appropriate cases, discharge his duty by taking reasonable steps to warn of the danger or to discourage persons from incurring the risk. Whether a warning is effective will depend among other things upon the nature of the risk and the age of the entrant.

The defence of *volenti non fit injuria* is preserved by s.1(6) of the Act. It is normally limited to dangers arising from the state of the premises. The plaintiff was held to have willingly accepted the risk as his own, within the meaning of s.1(6) of the Act in the case of *Rathcliffe v McDonnell* (CA 1999). In this case, the plaintiff, having drunk four pints agreed to go open-air swimming with his friends. He climbed over the gate of a college swimming pool. Although conscious of a warning sign he dived in the pool and suffered horrific injuries as a result.

The Court of Appeal rejected his claim for damages on the grounds that he was aware of the risk and had willingly accepted it.

As far as the defence of *ex turpi* is concerned, it was held in *Revill v Newberry* (CA 1996) that the fact that the plaintiff was a burglar did not take him outside the protection of the law, so that he was entitled to succeed in negligence when the defendant unintentionally shot him. There was, unsurprisingly, a substantial reduction in damages for contributory negligence.

Exclusion notices

There is no mention in the Act of excluding liability to the non-visitor, and the provisions of the Unfair Contract Terms Act 1977 do not apply to the 1984 duty. Trespassers pose problems because depending upon the point at which they enter the premises, they may be less likely to see a notice than a lawful visitor.

One suggested solution is that the duty under the 1984 Act is a minimum which cannot be excluded so that even the lawful visitor would be protected by it, even though he was aware of an exclusion notice.

Independent contractors and trespassers

At common law, the liability of a contractor to the trespasser rests upon ordinary negligence principles. The fact that the claimant is a trespasser in relation to the occupier is not relevant except in so far as the trespassers presence may be less foreseeable. One case which illustrates this is *Buckland v Guildford Gas Light and Coke Co* (HC 1949). The defendants, who had erected electricity cables on a farmer's land close to the top of a tree, were held liable for the death of a young girl who climbed the tree and was electrocuted.

Breach of statutory duty

Breach by the defendant of an obligation under statute (other than one which expressly seeks to impose liability in tort) may, apart from giving rise to any criminal sanction laid down in the Act, also enable a person injured by the breach to bring a civil action for damages for breach of statutory duty. This is a tort in its own right independent of any other form of tortuous liability. Whether a claimant can sue depends on whether the statute confers a right of civil action, or can be interpreted as conferring this right.

The claimant must prove that the legislature intended to create a right to sue. In *Cullen v Chief Constable of the Royal Ulster Constabulary* (2003) the House of Lords upheld the previous decisions that the claimant could not rely on the tort of breach of statutory duty for the failure of the police to give him reasons for delaying his access to a solicitor, on the ground that the duty concerned could be enforced through judicial review. In a few instances, Parliament has expressly made known its intention, but in the majority of cases statute is silent on the issue. It is for the courts to decide what the intention of an Act is and, to this end, certain guidelines have been established. The basic proposition is that a breach of statutory duty does not, by itself, give rise to a private law action. Such an action will arise, however, if it can be shown that, on the proper construction of the statute, the duty was imposed for the protection of a limited class of the public and Parliament intended to confer upon members of that class a right to sue for breach. There is no general rule for determining whether the Act does create such a right, but if no other remedy is provided for its breach that is an indicator in the claimant's favour. If the Act does contain other provision for enforcing the duty that is an indication of an intention that it was to be enforced by those means alone and not by private law action.

In determining whether, in any particular case, a civil action for breach of statutory duty will lie, the starting point is to look at precedent or for a clearly stated Parliamentary intention. In the absence of either it is in all cases a question of ascertaining the fundamental purpose the legislation intended to achieve, and that can only be done through a consideration of the Act as a whole.

The elements of the tort-Duty owed to the claimant

In establishing that breach of the particular duty will, in principle, ground a right of action, the claimant will, in most cases, have established that the obligation was imposed for the benefit of a limited class. The claimant must then prove that he is a member of that class.

In the case *Hartley v Mayoh and Co* (CA 1954) the widow of a fireman electrocuted while fighting a fire at the defendant's factory had no cause of action because the regulations existed for the benefit of "persons employed" and her husband was not so employed.

Defendant and breach of duty

The claimant must prove that the claimant was in breach. This can only be ascertained by having regard to the precise wording of the Act to determine the nature of the obligation. Some obligations are absolute, such as those contained within health and safety Acts.

Damage of the contemplated type

For the claimant to succeed the harm suffered must be of a type which the act was designed to prevent. In the case, *Gorris v Scott* (1874) the plaintiffs sheep were swept overboard the defendant's vessel during a storm. The sheep were not penned, contrary to statutory regulations, but the plaintiff failed in his action because the object of the regulations was to prevent the spread of disease, not to afford protection from the dangers of the sea. Another case illustrating this is *Donaghey v Boulton and Paul Limited* (HL 1968) where the plaintiff slipped and fell through an open space in an asbestos roof on which he was working. In breach of their duty the defendants had failed to provide him with adequate crawling boards, but argued that the object of the regulations was to prevent workers from falling through fragile roofing materials, not through holes in the roof. This argument was rejected and the House of Lords held the defendant's liable.

Causation

The burden rests upon the claimant to prove on a balance of probabilities that the breach of statutory duty caused or materially contributed to the damage. In this respect there is no distinction between this tort and a common law negligence action, so that the claimant must show that he would not have been injury were it not for the defendant's breach. The claimant must also show that the damage is not too remote and the usual test of reasonable foresight applies.

A problem arises where the claimant's own wrongful act puts the defendant in breach. In *Ginty v Belmont Building Supplies Ltd* (HC 1959) a regulation binding upon both parties required the use of crawling boards on a fragile roof. The defendant had provided the boards and given full instructions to the plaintiff how to use them. The plaintiff neglected to use them and fell through the roof. Both parties were clearly in breach of their statutory obligation but it was held that the plaintiff was the sole cause of his injury and his action failed.

Even if the claimant is in breach of his statutory duty he will fail in his action if it is his own deliberate folly which puts the defendant in breach. However, this will be mitigated by the actions of the defendant if he is also in breach.

****

2.4

Negligence-Liability for Defective or Dangerous Products

Part 1 of the Consumer Protection Act 1987, which came into force on 1st March 1988, creates a strict liability for dangerous goods.

Part 1 was enacted to give effect to an E.C. Directive of 1985, requiring the harmonisation of law on product liability throughout the E.C. If the Act doesn't apply in certain circumstances a claimant may still be able to sue for negligence. When claiming damages for harm suffered as a result of a defective product, the claimant must prove that he or she suffered damage caused wholly or partly by a defect arising from a specific product.

The Act (s.2.(2)) outlines who the potential defendants might be in such cases:

- the producer of the product;
- any person who holds himself out to be a producer by putting his name or trade mark or any other distinguishing mark on the product;
- an importer of the product into a Member State from a place outside the E.C. in order to supply it to another in the course of his business.

The term 'producer' is defined in s.1(2) to mean either the manufacturer, or the person who won or extracted the product, or, where the product has not been manufactured, won or abstracted but the essential characteristics of which are attributable to an industrial or other process having been carried out, the person who carried out that process.

Furthermore, by s.2(3) the mere supplier (e.g. Retailer) is liable if he fails within a reasonable time to comply with the plaintiff's request to identify one or more of the persons to whom s.2(2) applies, or to identify his own supplier.

'Product' is defined in s.1(2) as any goods or electricity. Component parts and raw materials also fall within the definition of product as distinct from the overall product in which they are comprised. For example, the brakes in a car would be the responsibility of both manufacturer of brakes and the supplier of the finished car.

The meaning of 'defect'

A product is defective, according to s.3(1) if its safety is not such as persons are generally entitled to expect. The safety of a product expressly includes safety "with respect to products comprised within that product" (i.e. components and raw materials) and a product may be unsafe not only if there is a risk of personal injury but also if it poses a risk of damage to property. When determining what people are entitled to expect, s.3(2) provides that account shall be taken of all the circumstances including the following specific matters:

- the way in which and the purposes for which the product has been marketed, its get-up, and warnings and instructions for use accompanying it:
- what might reasonably be expected to be done with or in relation to the product;

118

- the time when the product was supplied by its producer to another.

The reference in (a) to the purposes for which the product has been marketed may indicate that a balance has to be struck between known risks associated with a product and the benefits which it seeks to confer. With regard to (b), a product which is clearly intended for a particular use may not be defective if it causes damage when put to an entirely different use. With (c) it is the time of supply by the producer to another which is relevant not the time of supply to the consumer.

Liability under the Act is considerably stricter that under common law. One case that illustrates this is *A and others v National Blood Authority* (2001). The claimants had been infected with Hepatitis C, through blood transfusions which had used blood products obtained from infected donors. The defendants argued that the product was as safe as might be expected, and also that the defect in the particular transfusion could not have been detected). Given the strict liability under the Act, it was held that factors which would have been relevant in a negligence action were completely irrelevant and the defendants were found to be liable under the Consumer Protection Act.

Definition of "damage"

Section 5(1) defines damage for the purposes of Part 1 as death or personal injury, or loss of or damage to property (including land), although claims for damage to property are limited in several respects. First, the defendant will not be liable for damage to the defective product itself, nor for damage to any product supplied with a defective component comprised in it. Secondly, there is no liability unless, at the time of the damage, the property was "of a description of property ordinarily intended for private use, occupation of consumption" and was intended by the claimant mainly for such purposes (s.5(3)). A person who suffers damage to his business property must therefore sue in negligence as opposed to under the Act.

Defences

Section 4(1) of the Act provides for defences as follows:

- The defect is attributable to compliance either with a domestic enactment or community law.

- The defendant did not at any time supply the product to another. A broad definition is given to "supply" in a later part of the act to include not only the usual types of supply contract but also gifts.

- The defendant supplied the product otherwise than in the course of his business and either he does not fall within s.2(2) (he is not a producer, "own brander" or importer) or he does so only by virtue of things done other wise than in a view to profit.

- The defect did not exist at the relevant time. By s.4(2) the "relevant time" means, in relation to electricity, the time at which it was generated. With all other products it means, in the case of a defendant to whom s.2(2) applies the time when he supplied the product to another and, in the case of a supplier, the time of the last supply by a person who is within the ambit of that section.

- The state of scientific and technical knowledge at the relevant time was not such that a producer of products of the same description as the product in question might be expected to have discovered the defect if it had existed in his products while they were under his control. This is called the "development risk" or "state of the art" defence

The defect constituted a defect in a product containing the defendant's component part (or raw material) and was wholly attributable to the design of the overall product or to compliance by the defendant with instructions given by the producer of the overall product.

Common law negligence

Where the Consumer Protection Act does not apply, the claimant must rely on existing common law remedies. If the claimant acquires defective goods under a sale or similar supply contract the remedy is to sue the supplier for breach of implied undertakings relating to quality. Although these contractual obligations are generally imposed only upon those who supply in the course of business, they are strict and entitle the claimant to recover both in respect of goods which simply fail to work or which are less valuable than those contracted for, and where the defect causes personal injury or damage to property. If the claimant does not have a contract, an action in tort may be pursued.

The duty of the manufacturer

The duty owed by a manufacturer to the consumer was stated in Donoghue v Stevenson (Hl 1932) by Lord Atkins as follows:

"A manufacturer of products, which he sells in such a form as to show that he intends them to reach the ultimate consumer in the form in which they left him with no reasonable possibility of immediate examination, and with the knowledge that the absence of reasonable care in the preparation or putting up of the products will result in an injury to the consumer's life or property, owes a duty to the consumer to take that reasonable care".

The term "products" includes not only comestibles, but many other diverse products such as shoes, vehicles, toys and so on. the manufacturer's duty extend to the packaging of the product and to any labels, warnings or instructions for use which accompany it. If the manufacturer of a finished product incorporates a component made by another, he is under a duty to check on its suitability and may be liable for failure to do so should it turn out to be defective. Where products are already in circulation when the defect is discovered the manufacturer must take reasonable steps to warn of the danger or to recall the products.

Manufacturer and ultimate consumer

The term "manufacturer" has been interpreted to include any person who actively does something to the goods to create the danger, such as assemblers, servicers, repairers, installers and erectors.

In *Malfroot v Noxal Limited* (HC 1935) an assembler was held liable when the side car which he had negligently fitted to a motor cycle came adrift and injured the plaintiff. Mere suppliers may come within the rule, even though they may be unaware of the danger and do nothing to create it. In the case *Andrews v Hopkinson* (HC 1957) a second hand car dealer was liable for failing to check that an 18 year-old car was roadworthy, with the result that the plaintiff was injured in a collision caused by a failure of the steering.

Apart from the end user of the product, the "ultimate consumer" is any person who may foreseeably be affected by it. In the case *Stennet v Hancock and Peters* (HC 1939) the defendant was held liable for negligently fitting a metal flange to a wheel of a lorry, so that it came off when the vehicle was in motion and struck the plaintiff.

Proof of negligence and damage

The burden rests upon the claimant as in any other negligence action. However, damage caused by a defect in manufacture as opposed to a defect in design, may easily give rise to an inference of negligence. On the other hand, if it is equally probable that the defect arose after the manufacturing process and is wholly unconnected with anything that the manufacturer may have done, claimant will fail.

The defendant will no longer escape liability however, merely by showing that he had a fool-proof system of manufacture and quality control, because the very fact of the defect may be evidence of negligence in the operation of that system by a person for whom the defendant is vicariously liable. Where the alleged defect is in relation to the design of the product, the claimant may face greater difficulty in that the issue of negligence is to be judged in the light of current knowledge which must be proved to have been such as to render the damage foreseeable.

As far as damage is concerned, liability only exists in respect of personal injury or damage to other property, although consequential financial loss is also recoverable. Pure economic loss is, however, irrecoverable.

****

Ch. 3

Business Law-Employment Law Contracts

Into every contract of employment are implied a number of obligations in so far as these are not inconsistent with the express terms of the individual contract of employment. These duties are based on principles developed by the courts in the decided cases.

Implied duties may be classified as follows:
a) to be ready and willing to work;

b) to use reasonable care and skill;

c) to obey lawful orders;

d) to take care of the employers property;

e) to act in good faith.

To be ready and willing to work
The fundamental duty owed to an employer by an employee is to be turn up to work and to work at the direction of the employer in return for wages. Two interesting cases have arisen in relation to this. In Miles v Wakefield Metropolitan District Council (1987) M was a superintendent registrar of births deaths and marriages, working 37 hours per week, three of which were on Saturday morning. As part of industrial action, M refused to carry out marriages on Saturday mornings, although he was willing to do his other work. Wages were deducted, M sued for lost wages and the employer won, with the House of Lords (Supreme Court) saying

that where an employee refuses to perform the full range of duties and had been told that he would not be paid if he did not, then the employers were entitled to withhold the whole of his remuneration, (3hrs) although he attended for work and carried out a substantial part of his duties.

To use reasonable care and skill

This has two aspects:

a) The duty not to be unduly negligent.

b) The duty to be reasonably competent.

If an employee is negligent during the course of his work, he may be regarded as being in breach of contract. In Lister v Romford Ice and Cold Storage Ltd (1957) a lorry driver, employed by the company, carelessly reversed his lorry and injured a fellow employee, who was his father. The employers paid damages to the father but claimed indemnity from the son, because of negligence. This was held to be the case.

Duty to be reasonably competent

If an employee is incompetent this may be a breach of contract. In Hamer v Cornelius (1858) this was held to be the case.

To obey lawful orders

An employee is under a duty to obey all the lawful orders of his employer, i.e. those which are within the scope of the contract. In Price v Mouat (1862) a lace salesman was ordered to card (pack) lace but he refused and was dismissed without notice. He claimed wrongful dismissal and this was held because the order was not one which was within the scope of his contract.

An employee, therefore, is not obliged to do any act, which is deemed to fall outside the ambit of his individual contract of employment. The question of the introduction of new technology has caused problems here and must be linked to the scope of managerial prerogative in introducing new work techniques. In Cresswell v Board of Inland Revenue (1984) the Revenue wished to introduce a computer system to assist with the PAYE system. The majority of the work associated with the system had been done manually. Did the employers have the ability to change the nature of the working system? Did the employers have the ability to change the nature of the working system? Held: employees were expected to adopt the new methods and techniques in performing their contracts if the employer provided the necessary training in new skills.

To take care of employers property

An employer is under an obligation to take reasonable care of his employer's property. In Superflux v Plaisted (1958) the defendant had been in charge of a team of vacuum cleaner salesmen and had negligently allowed fourteen cleaners to be stolen from his van. Held: he was in breach of his contract of employment.

To act in good faith

His implied duty has several different aspects, which together form the basis of a relationship of trust. There is the duty not to make a secret profit, i.e. not to accept bribes.

This principal was clear from the case of Reading v AG (1951) which concerned a member of the armed forces, in which Lord Normand said: ---though the relation of a member of his majesty's forces is not accurately described as that of a servant under a contract of service--he owes to the Crown a duty as full fiduciary as the duty of a servant to his master--and in consequence--all profits and advantages gained by the use of his military status are to be for the benefit of the Crown'.

Duty to disclose certain information.

There appears to be no general duty on an employee to inform his employer of his misconduct and deficiencies: Bell v Lever Brothers (1932). However, there is one important exception, namely where the employment of that particular person is made more hazardous by virtue of an undisclosed defect on part of the employee.

Covenants in restraint of trade

A covenant in restraint of trade is a clause in a contract, which purports to limit an employees rights to seek employment when and where he chooses upon leaving his employment. This is usually done as a protective measure by an employer when he might suffer as a result of disclosure of confidential information or for other such reasons.

There are difficulties however, in enforcing such covenants and the employer has to demonstrate that the covenant is justified. A court will look at such factors as the time that the covenant runs, geographical area that it covers and public interest when considering the reasonableness of such covenants.

If a covenant is found to be unreasonable, the contract as a whole is not necessarily regarded as void, unless it is impossible to distinguish the covenant from the rest of the contract. If the covenant can be severed from the rest of the contract, without altering the nature of the agreement, the unreasonable clause may be struck out: see Commercial Plastics LTD v Vincent (1965).

If an employer breaks the contract of employment by wrongfully dismissing an employee, the employee may disregard any covenant in the contract which purports to limit his right to seek employment elsewhere: see General Billposting v Atkinson (1909).

Patents

At common law, unless the contract dealt with the matter, an employee would not normally be entitled to the benefit of any invention made by him if to allow him to do so would be a contravention of the implied duty of the employee to act in good faith.

The Patents Act 1977 (as amended), ss-39-47, gives ownership of an invention to the employee inventor unless the invention was made in the course of the duties for which he was employed. Any disputes are dealt with by the patents court.

Duties of the employer

By virtue of common law, and a number of statutory provisions, employers have a considerable number of obligations towards employees. The main examples are:

To pay contractually agreed remuneration

An employer is under no obligation to provide work as long as remuneration is paid. This however, has been questioned in recent times, particularly in relation to skilled employees. Lord Denning said, in Langston v AUEW (1973): 'In these days an employer, when employing a skilled man, is bound to provide him with work. By which I mean that the man should be given the opportunity of doing his work when it is available and when he is ready and willing to do it'. Therefore, a failure to provide work of a nature that the employee is used to could be regarded as constructive dismissal.

There are three exceptions to the rule, one is piecework, the second is where the nature of the employment is such that the actual performance of the work forms part of the consideration supplied by the employer, the employee may be entitled to compensation over and above the contractual wages. These situations are sometimes referred to as 'names in lights' clauses. the other exception is when an employee is taking part in limited industrial action.

To pay the National Minimum Wage and National Living Wage

The National Minimum Wage (NMW) is the minimum pay per hour most workers in the UK are entitled to by law. The rate varies depending on age and whether a person is an apprentice. Most workers who are 25 or older must be paid at least the National Living Wage (NLW), which is the highest rate of the National Minimum Wage.

National Minimum Wage and National Living Wage Rates for 2019/20 and 2020/21

Age	Minimum hourly rate 2019-20	2020/21
25 and over	£8.21	£8.72
21 to 24	£7.70	£8.20
18 to 20	£6.15	£6.45
Under 18	£4.35	£4.55

Age	Minimum hourly rate 2019-20	2020/21
Apprentice	£3.90	£4.15

Apprentices and the National Minimum Wage
Apprentices are entitled to the apprentice rate of the National Minimum Wage if they are either:

- Under 19
- 19 or over and in the first year of their apprenticeship

- Apprentices over 19 who have completed the first year of their apprenticeship are entitled to the National Minimum Wage for their age.

Entitlement to the National Minimum Wage
A person must be at least school leaving age (the last Friday in June of the school year in which the person turns 16) to get the National Minimum Wage. Almost all workers are entitled to the National Minimum Wage, including:

- Casual workers
- Part-time workers
- Temporary workers

There are some types of workers who don't qualify:
- self-employed people running their own business
- company directors
- volunteers or voluntary workers

- workers on a government employment programme, such as the Work Programme
- members of the armed forces
- family members of the employer living in the employer's home
- non-family members living in the employer's home who share in the work and leisure activities, are treated as one of the family and are not charged for meals or accommodation, for example au pairs
- workers younger than school leaving age (usually 16)
- higher and further education students on a work placement up to 1 year
- workers on government pre-apprenticeships schemes
- people on the following European Union programmes: Leonardo da Vinci, Youth in Action, Erasmus, Comenius
- people working on a Jobcentre Plus Work trial for 6 weeks
- share fishermen
- prisoners
- people living and working in a religious community

Work experience and internships
A person will not get the National Minimum Wage or National Living Wage if they are:

- a student doing work experience as part of a higher or further education course
- of compulsory school age
- a volunteer or doing voluntary work
- on a government or European programme
- work shadowing

Voluntary work

A person is classed as doing voluntary work if they can only get certain limited benefits (for example reasonable travel or lunch expenses) and they are working for a:

- charity
- voluntary organisation or associated fund-raising body
- statutory body

How the National Minimum Wage and National Living Wage are calculated

Deductions from your pay before National Minimum Wage is calculated: If an employee has paid for certain things related to their job out of their wages, the employer should deduct these payments before they calculate whether they have been paid the correct minimum wage. These payments are:

- Payments for the employer's own use or benefit - for example, if they have paid for travel between work sites
- Payments for things needed for the job but aren't refunded for – such as tools, uniform or equipment
- All other payments made out of wages, such as tax and National Insurance, should be included when the employer calculates whether the employee has been paid the National Minimum Wage.

Minimum wage for different types of work – and what counts as working time

The National Minimum Wage is worked out as an hourly rate, but it applies even if the employee is not paid by the hour.

Accommodation and the National Minimum Wage

If an employer provides accommodation, they can take the value of this into account when calculating the National Minimum Wage or National Living Wage. No other company benefit (such as childcare vouchers, meals, or a car) counts towards the National Minimum Wage or National Living Wage.

What doesn't count towards the National Minimum Wage

An employee might be paid at a higher rate than their standard pay rate for some of the work they do – for example for working:

- overtime, weekend or night shifts
- on bank holidays
- longer than a certain number of hours.

If the employee is, the premium element of pay – that is, the amount the higher pay rate exceeds the basic rate – does not count towards their minimum wage pay. The employer also cannot count the following towards the minimum wage pay:

- tips or gratuities
- service charges
- cover charges from customers.

However, an employer can include incentive payments or bonuses as part of the basic pay.

What to do if you think you've been paid less than the correct minimum wage

If you think you've been paid less than the correct minimum wage for your age, talk to your employer directly.

If this doesn't solve the problem, you can ask to see your payment records and make copies of them. You can contact the ACAS helpline for free, confidential advice to help you solve your payment dispute. You can also make a complaint to HMRC about your employer.

If HMRC find that you've been paid incorrectly, your employer must pay you any amounts they owe you and pay a fine to HMRC for paying below the minimum wage.

What is the Living Wage?
The Living Wage is set by the Living Wage Foundation. There is a UK rate and a London rate. The UK Living Wage is £8.75 an hour and the London Living Wage is £10.20 an hour. The Living Wage is based on the cost of living. The Resolution Foundation (a think tank that aims to improve the living standards of low and middle-income families) calculates the rates, and is overseen by the Living Wage Foundation.

Employers don't have to pay the Living Wage, but over 3,600 employers choose to do so.

What's the difference between the National Living Wage and the Living Wage?
The National Living Wage:
- is the highest rate of the National Minimum wage (currently £7.83 an hour)
- is set by government
- must be paid to all workers over 25

The Living Wage:
- is set by the Living Wage Foundation
- applies to all worker over 18
- is voluntary – employers can choose whether to pay it
- has two rates – a UK rate (£9.30 an hour), and a London rate (£10.55 an hour) (current 2019/2020)

To treat employees with trust and confidence

In Courtaulds Northern Textiles Ltd v Andrew (1978) the EAT held'---there is an implied term in a contract of employment that employers will not, without reasonable and proper cause, conduct themselves in a manner calculated or likely to destroy or seriously damage the relationship of trust or confidence between the parties' A series of cases have firmly established this principle.

To observe provisions relating to holidays

The written statement provided to employees under the 1996 Act ought to state the holidays to which the employee is entitled and whether the employee is entitled to holiday pay and if so how much. There are relatively few statutory provisions. Section 94 of the Factories Act 1961 provides that women and young persons who work in factories must have a holiday on bank holidays and the Wages Councils and Agricultural Wages Board have the power to fix holiday pay for workers in the industries over which they have jurisdiction.

To observe provisions relating to hours of work

The hours which an employee is required to work are determined by reference to his individual contract of employment and the written statement supplied to the employee ought to state these. There are certain statutory provisions, section 7 of the Sex Discrimination Act 1986 (now replaced by the Equality Act 2010) removed the majority of limitations imposed concerning the hours to be worked by women. Part V1 of the Factories Act 1961 limits the working day to no more than nine hours for young people.

In addition, see below, the Working Time Regulations 1998. These have introduced specific regulations controlling the working week and covers a broad variety of workers not only employees.

To permit employees time off work for public duties

The 1996 Act provides that an employer must permit an employee to have time off work for the purpose of carrying out work as:

a) Justice of the peace (work relating to this)

b) a member of a local authority

c) a member of a statutory tribunal

d) a member of a regional health authority or an Area or District educational establishment.

e) a member of a governing body of a local authority maintained educational establishment.

A number of categories of employees are excluded from this right, under the 1996 Act. Under the 1996 Act a pregnant employee has the right not to be unreasonably refused time off work with pay in order that she may keep appointments for receiving anti-natal care. Evidence of pregnancy and appointment must be produced if requested by employer.

To indemnify employees

An employer is under an obligation to indemnify his employees in respect of any expenses incurred in performing their duties under the contract of employment, for example traveling expenses. In certain circumstances however, the employee may be under an obligation to indemnify the employer for any loss sustained: see Lister v Romford Ice and Cold Storage LTD (1957)

To provide references

As we have seen in chapter one, there is no obligation on an employer to supply character references for employees although, in practice, employers normally supply them since failure to provide one speaks for itself. The legal effect of references means that if an employer does provide one, it ought to be correct for several reasons: If a reference is defamatory, the defamed employee may bring an action against the employer, although the defence of qualified privilege is available to the employer, i.e. the employer may show that the statements were made without malice.

Negligent misstatement. A person who acts in reliance on a reference, which has been issued negligently, may apparently bring an action to recover any loss sustained as a consequence.

Working Time Rights

Under Europe's Working Time Directive, most people now have seven basic rights to proper time off, rest breaks and paid holiday.

Who has working time rights?

These working time rights apply to all employees and workers from the first day of employment. The rights apply to most agency workers, homeworkers and freelancers. Only those who are self-employed and are genuinely running their own business do not have the right to paid annual leave.

Working time rights do not apply to:

- individuals who are self-employed and who are genuinely running their own business
- individuals who can choose freely their hours and duration of work (such as a managing executive)
- the armed forces, emergency services and police are excluded in some circumstances
- domestic servants in private houses

Working time rules also apply differently to some groups of workers (e.g. those who have to travel a long distance from home to get to work) and in some sectors or workplaces (e.g. security, hospitals, or air, road or sea transport) or when there is an emergency or accident.

Rest breaks

You have the right to a rest break of at least 20 minutes where you work for a continuous period of six hours or more during a working day / shift. If you are under 18 however, you are entitled to a 30-minute break after working four and a half hours.

Additional or longer breaks may be provided for in your contract. A lunch break or coffee break can count as a rest break. The requirements are:

- the break must be in one block
- it cannot be taken off one end of the working day - it must be somewhere in the middle
- you are allowed to spend it away from the workplace

Your employer can say when rest breaks can be taken provided they meet these requirements.

You do not have an automatic right to be paid for rest breaks. Whether you receive pay for rest breaks will depend on your contract.

Daily rest periods

You have the right to a rest period of 11 uninterrupted hours every working day. If you are under 18, you are entitled to a 12 hour uninterrupted rest period per working day. This rest period must be continuous and uninterrupted.

Weekly rest breaks

You have the right to a rest period of either:

- 24 hours in every 7 day period or
- 48 hours in every fortnight

This rest period must be continuous and uninterrupted. Employers have a duty to make sure that you take your breaks.

48 hour working time limit

You have the right not to work more than 48 hours a week on average. This limit is averaged over a 17-week period. This means that it is legal to work more than 48 hours in some weeks, so long as you work less in others.

You can opt out of this right unless you work at night, but should not be pressured to opt out. The opt-out must be voluntary and must be in writing.

You have a right to opt back in again to working time protection at anytime, but you must give your employer at least 7 days notice. You may be required to give more notice - up to 3 months, if you previously agreed to this with your employer in writing.

Young workers and working time limits

The weekly working time limits for young workers are 8 hours a day and 40 hours per week.

For the majority of young workers these are absolute limits. A young worker's working time is not averaged over a reference period, so in one week they must not work more than 40 hours. The opt-out provisions do not apply to young workers. Young workers will only be able to work more than 8 hours per day, or 40 hours per week if they are needed to:

- keep the continuity of service or production
- respond to a surge in demand for a service or product

And provided that:
- there is no adult available to do the work
- their training needs are not negatively affected

For further detailed information about your working time rights and how these can be enforced please see the TUC guide, 'Enforcing your Basic Workplace Rights'.

What counts as working time?
As well as time spent doing your job, your working time will include time spent on:

- job related training
- job related travelling time, although not time spent travelling
- overtime, whether paid or unpaid
- time spent 'on-call' at the workplace
- working lunches
- time spent working abroad if you work for a UK- based company

What does not count as working time?
Your working time does not include:
- breaks when no work is done, e.g. lunch breaks
- time when you are on-call away from the workplace (although time spent working when away from the workplace, e.g. answering calls at home, will count as working time)
- paid or unpaid holidays

Working in more than one job

If you work for more than one employer, the combined time that you work should not exceed more than 48 hours, unless you have signed the opt out with your employers.

Night work

Regular night workers should not work more than eight hours in each 24-hour period. The Working Time Regulations allow for night work to be averaged over a 17-week period in the same way as weekly hours of work. Please note that there is no opt out from the night work limits.

If your night work involves special hazards or heavy physical or mental strain, you cannot be made to work more than eight hours in any 24 hour period.

Young workers under 18 are not permitted to work between 10pm-6am.

Before night work can commence an employer must have offered you an opportunity to undertake a free health assessment unless you have previously had a health assessment which is still valid. Your employer must then offer you free health assessments at regular intervals, to ensure it is still safe for you to undertake night work. Where an employer is advised by a doctor/registered medical practitioner that you cannot undertake night work, the employer should where possible, transfer you to work which they are suited and is work within normal working time (day time).

It is good practice for your employer to provide you with enhanced pay rates for doing night work or unsocial hours. But you will not have a right to receive enhanced pay for doing night work, unless your contract provides for it.

What can I do if I am not allowed to take rest breaks or am asked to work excessive hours?

If your employer does not permit you to take rest breaks or daily or weekly breaks, you can make a complaint to an Employment Tribunal. If your employer pressurises you to work more than 48 hours when you have not signed an opt-out or does not comply with night work rules, you can make a complaint through the Pay and Work Rights helpline. It is always a good idea to seek advice from your union rep or from the ACAS Helpline before taking steps to enforce your rights.

Holiday pay

If you work regular hours and get the same pay each week, then holiday pay is simply the same as your normal pay. If your normal pay includes regular bonuses, shift premiums or contractual overtime payments, then these should also be included in your holiday pay.

If your weekly pay varies because your hours vary from week to week, then your weekly holiday pay should be the average weekly pay you earned over the last 12 weeks.

An interesting case relating to holiday pay is The Sash Windows Workshop Ltd v and Another v King (ECJ) 2015 where a salesperson agreed with his company that he would be self-employed, rather than be engaged on an employment contract. Crucially, this meant that he was not given annual leave. After he retired he claimed that he was owed 13 years backdated holiday pay because he was really a worker.

The case went to the ECJ, which concluded that the onus is on the employer to provide paid annual leave to individuals who are really 'workers' regardless of how they are labeled and whether or not the ask for paid leave.

Holiday pay paid throughout the year

When paid holidays were first introduced in 1998, some people found a change to their pay slip. Their take home pay was still the same, but now made up of two elements. First was their basic pay, which had been reduced from what it had been in previous pay packets. The difference was made up with a new element called holiday pay. The employer then said that there was no need for paid holidays as you were getting your holiday pay throughout the year and should save up for it.

Paying holiday pay in this way is now illegal in Scotland but still legal in England and Wales. However, the amount specified must be a genuine addition. See the next chapter for more about holiday pay entitlement.

Special hazards

If your work involves special hazards or heavy physical or mental strain, and you are a night worker, then you cannot work more than eight hours in any 24. This is not an average but an absolute limit.

****

3.2

Terminating Employment

There are a number of ways in which a contract of employment may come to an end-termination by way of contract, termination in breach of contract and termination by methods external to the contract.

At common law, a contract of employment can be validly terminated by an employer giving notice to an employee in accordance with the terms of the contract or, in the absence of such a term, by giving reasonable notice. If sufficient notice was given, the employee had no further rights and this meant that dismissal could be entirely arbitrary. However, in recent times provisions have been introduced whereby an employee may be entitled to compensation for loss of job despite the fact that he was given notice.

It should be noted that once notice has been given, it can only effectively be withdrawn with the consent of the other party.

Dismissal with notice

The length of notice, which must be given by an employer to an employee, is determined by reference to the following criteria to be applied in the following order:

a) Express terms of the contract. If the contract of employment expressly provides for a period of notice, this must be observed unless that period is less than the statutory minimum to which that particular employee is entitled under d) below.

b) In the absence of an express term it may be impossible to imply a term into the contract, for example, by custom. Again, such a period may not be less than the statutory custom.

c) If there is no express or implied term of the contract, the courts may rely on a reasonable period. What is "reasonable" depends upon such factors as the status of the employee, salary, length of employment with that employer, age etc. The "reasonable" period cannot be less than the statutory minimum. In the absence of any of the above criteria, or where they produce a period less than the following, the statutory minimum in s 86 of the 1996 Act (ERA) must be applied in respect of those employees covered by that section. Section 86 provides that for an employee continuously employed for between one month and two years, the notice period is one week; for an employee employed for more than two years, he is entitled to one week for each year of continuous employment subject to a maximum of twelve weeks notice after twelve years of employment. These rights do not apply to a contract for the performance of a specific task, which is not expected to last for more than three months.

Constructive dismissal

Constructive dismissal is when you're forced to leave your job against your will because of your employer's conduct.

The reasons you leave your job must be serious, for example, they:

- don't pay you or suddenly demote you for no reason
- force you to accept unreasonable changes to how you work – e.g. tell you to work night shifts when your contract is only for day work
- let other employees harass or bully you

Your employer's breach of contract may be one serious incident or a series of incidents that are serious when taken together. You should try and sort any issues out by speaking to your employer to solve the dispute.

If you do have a case for constructive dismissal, you should leave your job immediately - your employer may argue that, by staying, you accepted the conduct or treatment.

Summary dismissal

Summary dismissal is where an employer dismisses an employee without giving the employee the amount of notice to which that individual is entitled. If there is no justification, such dismissal is wrongful and an action can be brought.

The remedy for wrongful dismissal is damages representing the loss of wages during the period of notice that ought to have been given. In addition, wrongful dismissal may also be unfair dismissal within the meaning of the 1996 Act.

Circumstances which justify summary dismissal

The question of what justifies summary dismissal is not one that can be answered with a simple rule since each case must be decided according to the particular circumstances. However, a general principle has emerged that summary dismissal is justified if the conduct of the employee is such that it prevents further satisfactory continuance of the relationship. This was the finding in Sinclair v Neighbour (1967).

The status of the employee in question is a relevant consideration as is the fact that the employee has a history of misconduct as opposed to an isolated incident.

Dismissals Procedure

If the contract states that dismissal is to be according to an established pattern (e.g. that there will be two warnings before dismissal occurs) it is a breach of contract if the procedure is not observed. (Tomlinson v L.M.S Rly (1944). If the contract states that the dismissal may only occur for certain specified reasons, a dismissal is wrongful if the reason for the dismissal is other than specified in the contract.

However, it should be noted that the 2002 Employment Act introduced the obligation on an employer to include a statutory disciplinary and grievance procedure which must be in the contract or written terms and must be followed before any dismissal proceedings can take place.

Waiver of rights

If an employee's conduct justified a summary dismissal, the right must have been exercised within a reasonable time of the conduct, which allegedly justified the action since delay may amount to a waiver of the breach of contract.

Employee leaving

An employee is entitled to terminate employment at any time by giving the amount of notice required by the contract. If the employee is deemed to have been entitled to terminate employment by reason of the employer's conduct that may constitute a constructive dismissal and the fact that he gave notice makes no difference.

If an employer's attitude causes an employee to terminate his contract without notice, this may well constitute constructive dismissal and the employee may act accordingly.

Termination by agreement

The parties to a contract of employment as with any other contract, may terminate their relationship by agreement at any time upon such terms as they may agree, e.g. payment of money as a golden handshake. It should be noted that a termination by agreement is not a dismissal for the purposes of the redundancy and unfair dismissals provisions of the 1996 Act. However, the tribunals are concerned to ensure that any alleged agreement to terminate a contract of employment is real and not merely a result of pressure imposed on an employee who is unaware of the significance of agreeing to terminate the contract and who faces dismissal as an alternative to so agreeing.

Termination by frustration

Frustration occurs whenever the law recognises that without default of either party a contractual obligation has become incapable of being performed because the circumstance in which performance would be called for would render it a thing different from that which was undertaken by the contract (Lord Radcliffe in Davis Contractors v Fareham UDC (1956)).

In the context of a contract of employment, the term frustration means that circumstances have arisen, without the fault of either party, that make it impossible for the contract to be performed in the way that may be reasonably expected and the contract automatically terminates without the need for notice to be given. Frustration of the contract is not deemed to be dismissal for legislative purposes. Examples of frustration may be sickness. In Notcutt v Universal Equipment Co (1986), a worker with 27 years service, who was two years from retirement suffered a permanently incapacitating heart attack. The court decided that this rendered performance of the contract impossible and therefore the contract was frustrated as he was unable to perform his obligation to work. The employee was therefore not entitled to sick pay during his period of notice.

Imprisonment is another example, however this has caused problems. In 1986, the Court of Appeal allowed a four year apprenticeship contract to be frustrated by a six months Borstal sentence: FC Shepherd LTD v Jerrom (1986). In this case court held that such a period of imprisonment made the performance of the contract impossible. As with the sickness, the courts will tend to look at each case on its own merits without applying hard and fast rules.

Action for wrongful dismissal

An employee who has been wrongfully dismissed may bring an action for damages against his former employer representing the amount of wages owed to him in respect of work already done and in respect of wages that the employee would have earned had he been given the amount of notice to which he was entitled. The amount of wages lost is determined by the ordinary principles of common law and includes all sums connected with the job, such as loss of tips etc. Damages for wrongful dismissal cannot normally include compensation for injured feelings or pride or the fact that future earnings may be affected.

The object of damages is to compensate the injured party for what he actually lost, not to punish the party in breach of contract, and therefore the courts have developed principles to ensure that the employee who has been wrongfully dismissed receives compensation only for his actual loss.

In the case of *Brighton & Sussex University Hospitals NHS Trust v Akinwunmi*, 2017, Mr Akinwunmi ('Mr A') was a consultant neurosurgeon for the NHS trust. Mr A had poor relationships with a number of fellow surgeons, and had previously complained that he was being bullied - and bought a race discrimination claim to the Employment Tribunal, which was settled. It had been agreed that Mr A would take an unpaid three month sabbatical. During this sabbatical, Mr A raised some concerns about patient safety and alleged that his colleagues were turning away NHS patients whilst accepting private work. His colleagues claimed that he was incompetent and his practices were unsafe. A complaint was made to the police that Mr A had also threatened to assault one of his colleagues. The police decided to take no further action - but the Trust failed to notify Mr A of this.

A decision was made to limit his sabbatical to three months, Mr A appealed against this decision but his appeal was not upheld, and his absence from work became unauthorised. Mr A argued that it was impossible for him to return to work as there were various serious outstanding issues with his colleagues and this could be a risk to patient safety. Mr A was also concerned the police might arrest him if he returned to work and came into contact with the colleague he was alleged to have threatened. The Trust stated that the complaints could not be dealt with *until* he returned. A disciplinary hearing was held and Mr A was dismissed because of his unauthorised absence. Mr A brought claims for unfair dismissal, automatic unfair dismissal because of whistleblowing and victimisation.

The ET dismissed Mr A's claims for whistleblowing and victimisation but did find that his dismissal was unfair. On appeal the Employment Appeal Tribunal agreed that dismissing Mr A for his unauthorised absence was unfair because the full context of the absence was not taken into consideration by the Trust.

The EAT held it was unreasonable for the Trust to expect Mr A to return to work before trying to resolve the outstanding issues and improve working relationships. The EAT agreed that insisting Mr A return to a workplace where people's lives could depend on good working relationships was particularly unreasonable. The EAT noted that the Trust's witnesses were found to be 'disingenuous' when giving evidence.

Damages against employee

Where an employee fails to give sufficient notice to his employer, the employer may sue the employee for damages representing the loss, which follows from the breach of contract. In practice, such actions are infrequent because the loss is often minimal.

Specific performance

Specific performance is an order from the court directing that the parties to a contract perform their contractual obligations. It is a fundamental principle of labour law that specific performance is granted to compel performance of a contract of employment and this principle is now embodied in s 235 of the Trade Union and Labour Relations (Consolidation) Act 1992.

Injunction

An injunction is an order from a court forbidding certain conduct, e.g. the breaking of a term of the contract of employment. Hence it may be used to prevent a breach of a covenant restraining an employee from taking employment with a rival of his former employer. The courts usually refuse to grant an injunction if it compels performance.

By virtue of the Trade Union and Labour Relations Act 1992, no court may issue an injunction if the effect of such an order would be to compel an employee to do any work or to attend any place to work.

However, where the injunction compelling performance is to the benefit of the employee, the court may be prepared to grant such an order. In Hill v CA Parsons LTD (1972) the defendant employers wished to enter into an agreement with an organisation of workers whereby it was agreed that all employers in certain sections, including the plaintiff, would be obliged to join that organisation. This arrangement was legal at the time but under the Industrial Relations Act 1971 it would have been invalid. The plaintiff did not wish to join the organisation and he was dismissed with four weeks notice. The Court of Appeal held that he was wrongfully dismissed since he was entitled to at least six months notice and furthermore an injunction was awarded which prevented the employee from being dismissed until that time elapsed by which time he would have a remedy under the 1971 Act.

Declaration

A declaration is an order from the court, which simply determines the rights of the parties in the case. It has no binding force in itself and is not available to all employees being restricted to those persons whose employment is derived from statute.

Written statement of reasons for dismissal

An employee who has been continuously employed for 2 years who has been dismissed, subject to the statutory provisions of the 2002 Act and the following of a formal procedure, is entitled to receive, upon request, a written statement of the reasons for his dismissal. The employer must supply the reason in writing within 14 days of the request. A claim may be presented to an industrial tribunal by an employee that his employer has "unreasonably" refused to provide a written statement of the reasons for dismissal or that it is inadequate or untrue. The right to a written statement only arises where the employee has been dismissed by his employer.

Suspension

In accordance with the general principle that an employer fulfils his contractual obligations by paying wages in accordance with the contract of employment, he may suspend an employee on full wages without breach of contract. An employer may only suspend an employee without pay if the contract expressly or impliedly provided for this. If the contract does not so provide, it is a breach of contract. Therefore, an employee who is suspended without contractual authority may treat himself as dismissed and claim accordingly.

Unfair Dismissal

The present law relating to unfair dismissal is to be found in the Employment Rights Act 1996. The significance of the concept of unfair dismissal is that it represents a further, and most important, step towards recognising the property right, which an employee has in his job. Additionally, it is no longer possible for an employer to end a contract by simply giving notice and thereby totally discharging his responsibilities. The threat of dismissal is no longer quite so important since the employee has a remedy if the threat is implemented. The 1996 Act provides that, subject to certain specified exceptions, every employee has the right not to be unfairly dismissed. It should be noted that a complaint of unfair dismissal does not depend upon the employer having acted in breach of contract but simply that the employer has terminated the contract in circumstances which are unfair. Certain categories of employees are excluded: employees who, at the effective date of termination of the contract have been continuously employed for less than one year, *two years if employed after 6th April 2012*, persons over retiring age, persons employed in the police service, share fishermen, employees who ordinarily work outside Great Britain, employees employed on fixed term contracts and persons covered by a designated dismissals procedure agreement.

Dismissal

If an action for unfair dismissal is to succeed, the employee must first establish that he was dismissed within the meaning of the Act. The employee must establish constructive dismissal if alleged. The Act provides that:

"an employee shall be treated as dismissed by his employer if the contract under which he is employed by the employer is terminated by the employer whether it is so terminated by notice or without notice or where under that contract he is employed for a fixed term, that term expires without being renewed under the same contract or the employee terminates that contract, with or without notice, in circumstances such that he is entitled to terminate it without notice by reason of the employers conduct".

The Act refers to the concept of so-called "constructive' dismissal. If an employee leaves employment entirely voluntarily, there is no dismissal but if he leaves because of the employers conduct then it may be deemed "constructive"

The courts and tribunals have been concerned to define the circumstances in which an employee is entitled to regard himself as having been constructively dismissed. In Western Excavating LTD v Sharp (1978) the tribunals found that sufficiently unreasonable behaviour on the part of the employer entitled an employee to leave his job and claim constructive dismissal. However, the Court of Appeal rejected the unreasonableness test and established that the correct test is one based on strict contractual principles. Accordingly, an employee is only able successfully to argue constructive dismissal where the employer has breached the contract in such a way as to justify the employee in treating himself as discharged from further performance. The action of an employer may involve breach of an express or implied term.

When is dismissal unfair?

The expression "unfair dismissal" is in no sense a commonsense expression capable of being understood by the person in the street. Whether a dismissal is unfair is affected, but not conclusively determined, by whether one or both parties has broken the terms of the contract of employment. The employer cannot, in seeking to show that a dismissal was not unfair rely on alleged misconduct not known to him at the time of the dismissal. An otherwise fair dismissal is not automatically rendered unfair by a failure to give proper notice.

Reasonableness. It is for the employer to establish the reason for the dismissal. The tribunal must then satisfy itself as to whether the employer acted reasonably or unreasonably. The EAT laid down the following general principles in Iceland Frozen Foods v Jones (1982):

a) In applying the provisions of the 1996 Act a tribunal must consider the reasonableness of the employers conduct and not simply whether they (the members of the tribunal) consider the dismissal unfair.

b) In judging the reasonableness of the employer's conduct a tribunal must not substitute its own decision as to what was the right course to adopt for that of the employer.

c) In many cases there is a band of reasonable responses to the employees conduct within which one employer might take one view and another quite reasonably another.

d) The function of the tribunal is to determine whether in the particular circumstances the decision to dismiss fell within the band of reasonable responses, which a reasonable employer might have adopted. If the dismissal falls within the band it is fair. If it falls outside the band it is unfair.

In deciding whether an employer acted reasonably, the industrial tribunal is required to have regard to the provisions of the ACAS Code of Practice-Disciplinary Code of Practice and Procedures in Employment. In broad terms, this provides that the disciplinary rules and procedures ought to have been made known to each employee and that a disciplinary procedure ought to contain certain essential procedures. It should be noted that the maximum compensatory awards for unfair dismissal increased to £86,444 from April 2019.

Reasons for dismissal

There are five categories of reasons, which, if one is established by the employer, may make the dismissal fair provided that the tribunal is satisfied that the employer acted reasonably. These are as follows:

a) Capability or qualification
b) Conduct
c) Redundancy
d) Illegality of continued employment
e) Some other substantial reason.

In addition, an employer in certain circumstances, can dismiss an employee for reasons connected to pregnancy. Usually, it is automatically unfair to do so unless the employer can establish that at the effective date of termination, because of her pregnancy, she:
a) is or will have become incapable of adequately doing the work she is employed to do or: or
b) cannot or will not be able to do the work she is employed to do without a contravention (either by her or her employer) of a duty of restriction imposed by law.

In Brown v Stockton on Tees Borough Council (1988) the House of Lords (Supreme Court) held that if a woman was selected for redundancy because she is pregnant, such a dismissal is automatically unfair. Indeed, Lord Griffith stated that "it surely cannot have been intended that an employer should be entitled to take advantage of a redundancy situation to weed out his pregnant employer".

However, even where the circumstances of a and b above apply, the dismissal is still unfair if the employer has a suitable vacancy, i.e. appropriate for a pregnant woman to do and not substantially less favourable than her existing employment in relation to the nature, terms and place of employment, which he fails to offer her.

Another case highlighting unfair dismissal was that of Georgia O'Brian v Bolton St Catherine's Academy. Ms O'Brien's ordeal began in 2011 when she was assaulted by a pupil at Bolton St Catherine's Academy whilst assisting a colleague with a disruptive student. Her physical injuries were not long-lasting in comparison with her mental reaction, resulting in an absence from the school and subsequent termination of her employment in January 2013.

In March 2017, the Court of Appeal confirmed that the decision of the Employment Tribunal in November 2014 was correct and should stand. In 2014, the Employment Tribunal found that Ms O'Brien's condition amounted to a disability and that her termination of employment was discriminatory and unfair. The school went on to appeal the decision and in September 2015 the Employment Appeal Tribunal (EAT) allowed the school's appeal. However in March 2017, the Court of Appeal overturned the EATs decision.

Another interesting case was that of Michael Hayward v Chadwicks Butchers. Michael Hayward had worked for Noel Chadwick, described to Manchester Employment Tribunal as a small and well-respected butchers in Wigan, for seven and a half years before he was dismissed for recommending a discount from online retailer Fresh Meat Packs North West to his then-girlfriend on Facebook.

Hayward was subsequently dismissed for gross misconduct and breach of contract by father and son directors John and Paul Chadwick for 'advertising' what they believed to be a competitor and breaching the company's social media policy. The tribunal heard the pair, whose business did not have a formal HR function, had already decided to dismiss Hayward before they brought him into a disciplinary meeting in April 2016.

The 37-year-old said he was not issued a written or verbal formal warning, despite requesting one, nor was he given the opportunity to have someone with him at the meeting or given an explanation regarding his actions. As no appeal was arranged within a few weeks of his sacking, Hayward eventually lost confidence in Noel Chadwick and did not follow up the matter.

The tribunal also heard that Hayward had been 'pulled up' on his use of social media before he posted the offer, but there was no warning given to him that suggested such behaviour could lead to his dismissal.

Allowing Hayward's unfair dismissal claim, Judge Keith Robinson called Noel Chadwick "fanciful" for suggesting it experienced any financial or reputational loss because of the Facebook post.

"Hayward's misdemeanour, if one can call it that, was minor," the judge continued. "This is not an advertisement; this [matter] was a wholly mishandled dismissal root and branch. The claimant was dismissed summarily in a process that was reprehensible."

The judge awarded Hayward a £6,091 payout – £4,891 in lost wages and compensation, and £1,200 to reimburse his tribunal fees.

Three other recent interesting cases based around unfair dismissal are:

Genus and Kelly v Fortem Solutions Ltd 2018. Two repair contractors who were fired for gross misconduct after they were discovered to have used company vehicles for personal purposes were unfairly dismissed, While the pair were at fault for misusing the vans, the tribunal found their employer failed to thoroughly investigate the issue before dismissing them

Evans Nixon v Staffordshire South West Citixens Advice Bureau 2018 involved a long-standing CAB employee who had been dismissed for redundancy after a series of funding cuts. A selection exercise had been undertaken to determine who was made redundant, and the Claimant argued that she had been unfairly disadvantaged in the scoring process while less experienced colleagues had been retained. She also argued that her age and her disability (she suffers from a brain disorder called leukoencephalopathy) were factors in the CAB's decision to dismiss her.

The Employment Tribunal considered her case and found that the individual scores had not been discussed with her, and she also had not been given a chance to dispute the scores before the CAB had taken the decision to terminate her employment. On that basis, the Claimant's dismissal had been procedurally unfair. However, the Tribunal found that there was no disability or age discrimination.

Talon Engineering Ltd v Smith 2018. Mrs Smith worked for a motorcycle manufacturer, Talon Engineering Ltd, and sent an email to a company that Talon dealt with calling one of her colleagues an unpleasant name. Following an investigation in to her conduct, Mrs Smith was called to a disciplinary meeting but her Union rep was unable to attend on the allotted day. Several alternative dates were suggested by Mrs Smith and her rep, the first being 2 weeks ahead. Talon were not willing to delay the hearing to accommodate Mrs Smith's companion and so it went ahead in her absence. Mrs Smith was found to have committed gross misconduct and was summarily dismissed. She appealed and her appeal was rejected. Mrs Smith then brought a claim in the Employment Tribunal for unfair dismissal.

The Tribunal found that Talon had a potentially fair reason for dismissing Mrs Smith, i.e. conduct, but concluded that no reasonable employer would have refused a further short postponement of the disciplinary hearing and gone ahead in her absence. It was noted that the further delay to ensure Mrs Smith's attendance and grant her the opportunity to be heard and accompanied would have been a short one.

Talon appealed to the Employment Appeal Tribunal (EAT), however, the EAT upheld the finding of unfair dismissal. The EAT also considered the right to be accompanied under section 10 of the ERA 1996, which says that the employer must postpone the hearing to allow the employee's chosen companion to attend, if the proposed alternative is within 5 working days.

The EAT found that Talon appeared to believe that because Mrs Smith's union rep suggested dates which did *not* fall within 5 working days, they were not obliged to reschedule the hearing.

Dismissal for trade union reasons

References in this section are to the Trade Union and Labour Relations (Consolidation) Act 1992. Trade Union membership or activities. Except in exceptional cases, a dismissal is automatically unfair if the employee can establish that the principal reason for it was that the employer was, or proposed to become, a member of an independent trade union, or that the employee had taken or proposed to take part in the activities of an independent trade union at any appropriate time or that the employee was not a member of any or a particular trade union, or had refused or proposed to refuse to become or remain a member.

Other reasons for dismissal

An industrial tribunal cannot determine whether a dismissal was fair or unfair if it is known that at the date of dismissal the employer was conducting or instituting a lock out or the complainant was taking part in a strike or other industrial action, unless it is shown:

a) that one or more relevant employees of the same employer have not been dismissed: or

b) that any such employee has, before the expiry of the period of three months beginning with the employee's date of dismissal, been offered re-engagement and that the complainant has not been offered re-engagement.

National security

If an employee has shown to have been dismissed on grounds of national security, as evidenced by a certificate signed by or on behalf of a minister of the Crown, the tribunal must dismiss the complaint. In Council of Civil Service Unions v Minister for the Civil Service (1985) (the GCHQ case), the court held that the requirements of national security outweighed those of fairness when the minister decided to ban trade unions at GCHQ, without consultation with the trade unions. Workers who refused to give up their trade union membership were subsequently fairly dismissed.

Procedure

An employee who considers that he has been unfairly dismissed may present a complaint to the Central Office of Industrial Tribunals within three months of the effective date of termination or within such further period as the tribunal considers reasonable in a case where it is satisfied that it was not reasonably practicable for the complaint to be presented within a time period of three months. Where the dismissal is unfair (failure to offer re-engagement where the dismissal is connected with a lockout or strike) the time limit is six months from the date of dismissal. A copy of the application is sent to the employer as respondent. If the employer wishes to contest any aspect of the complaint, he must enter a "notice of appearance" within 14 days, although tribunals have a wide discretion to grant an extension of time. Once this has happened, a date is set down for the hearing of the case by an industrial tribunal.

Conciliation

A copy of the application is also sent to a conciliation officer. He is under a statutory duty, either at the request of the parties or on his own initiative, to endeavor to promote a voluntary settlement of the issue, either by way of an agreement to reinstate or re-engage the complainant or an agreement as to the payment of compensation in respect of the dismissal. there is no legal duty upon the parties to co-operate with the conciliation officer.

Pre-hearing Assessments

Under the Industrial Tribunals Regulations (S1 1985/16) provision is made for a pre-hearing assessment of the case to be made at the request of either of the parties or on the notion of the tribunal itself. At the tribunal, it is for the complainant to establish that he was dismissed (unless dismissal is conceded). It is then for the tribunal to satisfy itself as to whether the dismissal was fair or unfair in accordance with the principles stated above. If the dismissal is found to be unfair, the tribunal will consider the remedies, which may be awarded. An appeal, on a point of law only, lies from an industrial tribunal to the Employment Appeal Tribunal.

Remedies

Reinstatement and re-engagement orders. If the Tribunal finds the dismissal unfair, it must explain to the complainant the remedies available and ask if he wishes to be reinstated or re-engaged. If the employee indicates that this is his wish then the Tribunal must consider whether it is practicable for the employer to comply with such an order. If the employer complies, but not fully, with a reinstatement or re-engagement order then, unless the tribunal is satisfied that it was not practicable to comply with the order, an additional award of compensation must be made.

If a reinstatement or re-engagement order is made but not complied with at all or if no such order is made, the tribunal must make an award of compensation on the basis of the following:

a) basic award, amount of which is calculated in line with redundancy payments;

b) compensatory award, being an amount that the tribunal considers just and equitable in all the circumstances having regard to the loss suffered by the complainant in consequence of the dismissal in so far as the loss is attributable to action taken by the employer subject to a maximum limit.

****

3.3

Discrimination in the Workplace

The ability of employers to discriminate in the workplace has been steadily eroded. In 2010, the Equality Act came onto the statute books and was implemented in two stages, October 2010 and April 2011. The Act replaced nine previous pieces of legislation, bringing them all under one umbrella.

The main changes contained within the Equality Act 2010 are making pay secrecy gagging clauses unenforceable, putting restrictions on employers asking job applicants questions about disability or health, making employers responsible for protecting their staff from harassment by customers and allowing employment tribunals that find an employer has discriminated against an employee to make recommendations that could affect the whole workforce.

The Equality Act replaced the Equal Pay Act 1970, The Sex Discrimination Act 1975, the Race Relations Act 1976, The Disability Discrimination Act 1996, The Employment Equality (Sexual Orientation) Regulations 2003, The Employment Equality (Religion or Belief) Regulations 2003 and the Employment Equality (Age) Regulations 2006, the Equality Act 2006 and the Equality Act (Sexual Orientation) Regulations 2007. In most cases, the thrust of the Acts that were incorporated into the Equality Act 2010 have remained unchanged, but are now contained within the 2010 legislation.

Equal Pay

In broad terms, the Equal Pay Act 1970, which has now been replaced wholesale by the Equality Act 2010, was concerned with less favourable treatment of one person relative to another in respect of matters governed by the contract under which a person is employed whereas the Sex Discrimination act 1975 dealt with less favourable treatment in matters not governed by the contract, on grounds of sex and/or marital status.

The Equal Pay Act 1970 was influenced by the treaty of Rome and the effect of certain European Community Directives have been considerable in this area and have significant practical consequences for any applicant contemplating bringing an action alleging breach of the Equality Act 2010.

Article 119 of the Treaty of Rome provides that: "each member state shall maintain the application of the principle that men and women should receive equal pay for equal work. For the purpose of this article, pay means the ordinary basic or minimum wage or salary and any other consideration, whether in cash or kind, which the worker receives, directly or indirectly in respect of his employment from his employer. The Article is directly enforceable by individuals in the courts of member states of the EEC. The 2002 Employment Rights Act introduced the right of the employee to give the employer a questionnaire in order to ascertain whether or not the employer is actually paying and treating equally. The employer does not have to comply.

Sex Discrimination

The Equality Act 2010 makes it unlawful for an employer to discriminate against employees because of their sex. Sex discrimination against men is just as unlawful as sex discrimination against women. Also, it is unlawful for a woman to discriminate against another woman because of her sex, and for a man to discriminate against another man because of his sex.

165

There are four main types of discrimination.

Direct discrimination

Is when someone is treated differently and not as well as other people because of their sex. For example, advertising a job and stating it is better suited to female applicants. It breaks down into three different sorts of treating someone 'less favourably' because of:

- their own sex (ordinary direct discrimination)
- their perceived sex (direct discrimination by perception)
- their association with someone of a particular sex (direct discrimination by association).

Indirect discrimination

Can occur where a workplace rule, practice or procedure is applied to all employees, but disadvantages those of a particular sex. For example, a requirement that job applicants must be six feet tall could be met by significantly fewer women than men.

An employee or job applicant claiming indirect discrimination must show how they have been personally disadvantaged, as well as how the discrimination has or would disadvantage other employees of the same sex.

In some limited circumstances, indirect discrimination may be justified in law if it is necessary for the business to work. However, employers should note this can be a difficult process.

Harassment

This breaks down into three different types:

- 'unwanted conduct' related to a person's sex causing a distressing, humiliating or offensive environment for them
- 'unwanted conduct' of a sexual nature - this is sexual harassment

- less favourable treatment of an employee because they have rejected sexual harassment or been the victim of it.

An interesting case in relation to Sexual harassment is that of Ms M Podlecka v MYM Global Ltd 2018 **where** the Employment Tribunal held that the Claimant should be awarded over £15,000 in compensation after she was wrongfully dismissed and discriminated against. Ms Podlecka commenced employment with MYM Global Ltd on 21 December 2016 as a Cost Estimator. Ms Podlecka alleged that he following had occurred during the course of her employment:

- That she had been subjected to sex discrimination in the workplace by Moshe Genish, the owner of the business and her line manager – comments of a sexualised nature were made by him and Mr Genish also inappropriately touched her hand on a few occasions;
- That her colleagues had acted in a hostile manner towards her;
- That Claudiu Praj had subjected her to abusive language and made derogatory comments about her religion and how old she was
- That Mr Praj would treat her as a secretary and not in the same way as he would treat male colleagues
- On 8 August 2017 Ms Podlecka complained to Mr Genish about Mr Praj's conduct. He launched an informal investigation; Ms Podlecka felt that the investigation did not include her enough and so she went home.

On 9 August 2017 Ms Podlecka sent Mr Genish an email containing a formal grievance (which complained primarily about Mr Praj's conduct). On 11 August 2017 Mr Genish dismissed Ms Podlecka, calling her immature and stating that the workplace was not a kindergarten. Ms Podlecka subsequently made Employment Tribunal claims for sex discrimination, unlawful deduction from wages, and notice pay.

The decision of the Employment Tribunal

The Employment Tribunal gave default judgment in Ms Podlecka's claims, MYM Global Ltd having failed to have provided a response to the claim. The Employment Tribunal awarded Ms Podlecka the following sums as compensation for her successful claims:

£10,000 in respect of injury to feelings (in compensation for the sex discrimination claim)
£1,750 in respect of loss of earnings
£350 in respect of notice pay
£1,250 in respect of holiday pay

An uplift of 25% for failure to comply with the ACAS Code of Practice.

Victimisation
Treating an employee unfairly who has made or supported a complaint about sex discrimination.

Other considerations

In very limited circumstances, there are some jobs which can require that the job-holder is a man or a woman. This is known as an 'occupational requirement'. One example is where the job holder is likely to work in circumstances where members of one sex are in a state of undress and might reasonably object to the presence of a member of the opposite sex, such as in a bra-fitting service.

Making a claim of Sex discrimination

If an employee feels they been discriminated against, they will be able to bring a claim to an employment tribunal. However, as with all matters it's best they talk to their employer first to try to sort out the matter informally.

Sexual Orientation

The Equality Act 2010 makes it unlawful to discriminate against employees, job seekers and trainees because of their sexual orientation. For example, an employer not promoting an employee purely because they are gay is likely to be discrimination.

The Act defines Sexual orientation as:

- orientation towards people of the same sex (lesbians and gay men)
- orientation towards people of the opposite sex (heterosexual)
- orientation towards people of the same sex and the opposite sex (bisexual).

The law applies equally whether someone is a lesbian, gay man, heterosexual or bisexual.

There are four main types of sexual orientation discrimination.

Direct discrimination

Breaks down into three different sorts of direct discrimination of treating someone 'less favourably' because of:

- their actual sexual orientation (ordinary direct discrimination)
- their perceived sexual orientation (direct discrimination by perception)
- the sexual orientation of someone with whom they associate (direct discrimination by association).

Indirect discrimination

Can occur where there is a policy, practice, procedure or workplace rule which applies to all employees, but disadvantages people of a particular sexual orientation. An example of this could be a particular policy for maternity/paternity leave does not apply to same-sex couples. In some limited circumstances, indirect discrimination may be justified if it is what the law terms 'a proportionate means of achieving a legitimate aim'.

Harassment

When unwanted conduct related to sexual orientation has the purpose or effect of violating an individual's dignity or creating an intimidating, hostile, degrading, humiliating or offensive environment for that individual.

Victimisation

Is when an employee suffers what the law terms a 'detriment' - something that causes disadvantage, damage, harm or loss - because, for example, they have made or supported a complaint about sexual orientation discrimination.

'Coming out' at work

When someone tells other people about their sexual orientation this is known as 'coming out'. This process is personal and different for everyone. While many lesbian, gay and bisexual people are 'out' in their personal lives, they may not want to 'come out' at work.

If the employee is limiting who they tell, they also need to decide whether they want those people to keep the details of their sexual orientation confidential. If someone reveals a person's sexual orientation to others against that person's will, this may be seen as:

- harassment and/or
- a breach of the Data Protection Act (if details are stored as confidential data) and/or
- a breach of any of the employer's relevant regulations or policies.

Harassment because of Sexual orientation

Harassment because of sexual orientation can take many different forms. It could be a verbal or written comment, what somebody thinks is a 'joke', exclusion from conversations or activities, violence or the threat of violence.

An employee's complaint of this nature should be taken seriously and the employer should take care to listen to their concerns. It should also be mindful that this type of complaint can be difficult for the individual to discuss.

It is important for an employer to deal with this type of complaint, not only because of its legal obligations, but also because there could be knock-on effects. The employee being harassed might feel de-motivated and their productivity fall, or it might lead to them being absent from work through stress. A climate of harassment can also damage morale in the workplace.

An employer may benefit from having a specific policy setting out how it would deal with complaints about sexual orientation discrimination.

Sexual orientation and Religion or belief

The Equality Act has specific exemptions where employment is for the purpose of organised religion, such as being a Minister or otherwise promoting or representing the religion.

This means that some roles can be restricted to people of a particular sexual orientation. There can also be additional requirements related to sexual orientation, such as a requirement for gay men or lesbians to be celibate. Restrictions concerning religion can also apply to the protected characteristics of sex, gender reassignment, and marriage and civil partnership. Such a restriction only applies when:

• appointing a person who meets the requirement/s in question is a proportionate way of complying with the doctrines of the religion, or

• because of the nature or context of the employment, employing a person who does not meet the requirement/s would conflict with a significant number of the religion's followers' strongly-held religious convictions. The

171

requirement/s must be a proportionate way of avoiding such a conflict.

Making a claim of Sexual orientation discrimination

If an employee feels they have been discriminated against, they may be able to make a claim to an employment tribunal. However, it's best to talk to the employer first to try to sort out the matter informally, in order to minimise the negative effects on all parties involved.

Race Relations

The Equality Act 2010 makes it unlawful to discriminate against employees, job seekers and trainees because of race - this includes the different elements of colour, nationality, and ethnic or national origin. For example, this would include turning down the best applicant for a job because they are Nigerian and the employer feels they would not 'fit in' with the rest of the staff because they are all English

.

There are four main types of race discrimination.

Direct discrimination

Breaks down into three different sorts of direct discrimination of treating someone 'less favourably' because of:

- their actual race (direct discrimination)
- their perceived race (direct discrimination by perception)
- the race of someone with whom they associate (direct discrimination by association).

Indirect discrimination

Can occur where there is a policy, practice, procedure or workplace rule which applies to all workers, but particularly disadvantages people of a particular race. For example, a requirement for all job applicants to have GCSE Maths and English would discriminate against potential candidates educated in countries which don't have GCSEs, unless the employer accepted equivalent qualifications. In some limited circumstances, indirect discrimination may be justified if it is what the law terms 'a proportionate means of achieving a legitimate aim'.

Harassment

When unwanted conduct related to race has the purpose or effect of violating an individual's dignity or creating an intimidating, hostile, degrading, humiliating or offensive environment for that individual.

Victimisation

Unfair treatment of an employee who has made or supported a complaint about race discrimination.

Managing cultural differences at work

Employers and employees should be mindful that employees/colleagues will often come from different backgrounds, and aware that there may be cultural differences as a result, particularly regarding customs and values. They should be sensitive and respectful towards such differences. It is good practice for an employer to provide training for staff to establish a culture of respect in this area, and provide an understanding of what constitutes acceptable and unacceptable behaviours.

Managing languages at work

The increased movement of people around the world means it can be quite common for organisations to employ staff from many different countries or ethnic backgrounds. As a result, there may be employees for whom English is not their first language. Often, there may be a number of employees who originate from the same country or share a common language which is not English. However, an employer:

- can specify a language of operation, usually English, for business reasons. However, in Wales some jobs require the holder to speak both English and Welsh
- can insist on recruiting a job candidate who has skills in English necessary for the job, but it must not select based on assumptions about race, nationality, or ethnic or national origins. Again, in Wales some jobs require the holder to have skills in both English and Welsh necessary for the job
- should be wary of prohibiting or limiting the use of other languages within the workplace unless they can justify this with a genuine business reason.

Employing staff from abroad

As discussed in chapter 1, employers must check their employees are entitled to work in the UK, and should also ensure any necessary paperwork is correct and up to date. However, employers should ensure they are consistent in the checks they carry out. For example, just doing them for potential new recruits they assume are not British citizens, or not from the Channel Islands, the Isle of Man or Republic of Ireland, may be potentially discriminatory. Workers from European Union countries plus Switzerland, Iceland, Liechtenstein and Norway are also entitled to work in the UK.

Ethnic and national origins and religion

Employers and employees should also be mindful that some ethnic and national groups have devout religious beliefs. For example, Sikhs have their own religion and the majority of Poles are Catholic. It is unlawful to discriminate against employees because of their religion or belief, or lack of religion or belief.

Making a claim of race discrimination

If someone feels they have been discriminated against, they may be able to make a claim to an employment tribunal. However, it's best to talk to the employer first to try to sort out the matter informally, in order to minimise the negative effects on all parties involved.

Discrimination on the grounds of disability

The 2010 Equality Act covers Discrimination on the grounds of disability. It is against the law for an employer:

- to treat a person less favourably because they are disabled than someone without a disability would be treated in the same circumstances. This is called direct discrimination

- to discriminate against a person because of their connection with someone else who is disabled, for example, their partner or child. This is called discrimination by association

- to discriminate against a person indirectly for example by requiring something which applies to all their colleagues but which is much more difficult for them and for disabled people to meet

- to treat a person unfavourably because of something connected with their disability. For example, a worker is given night shifts to do. They have kidney failure and has nightly dialysis. Making them do night shifts would mean they wouldn't be able to have their dialysis

- not to make reasonable adjustments to the workplace to allow a person to work or to continue to work

- to harass a person if they are disabled, for example, by making jokes about their disability

- to victimise a person if they take legal action because of discrimination against them, or if they help someone else to take legal action because of discrimination

Employers can treat disabled people less favourably only if they have a sufficiently justifiable reason for doing so, and only if the problem cannot be overcome by making 'reasonable adjustments'. For example, an employer would be justified in rejecting someone with severe back pain for a job as a carpet fitter, as they cannot carry out the essential requirements of the job.

Examples of the types of adjustments that an employer might make include:

- making physical adjustments to the premises
- supplying special equipment to help a person do their job, or providing information in an accessible format
- transferring a person to a different post or workplace
- altering hours of work or giving extra time off

When employers are deciding whether an adjustment is reasonable they can take into account several things, including the cost of making an adjustment and the size of their business. If a person is already in the job, their employer can also take into account their skills and experience and the length of time they have worked there.

An interesting case relating to discrimination on the grounds of disability is Peninsula Business Systems v Baker 2017. In this recent case, the Claimant, Miss Baker, claimed that she suffered from Dyslexia. This was confirmed by a psychologist's report.

The Respondent, Peninsula, were concerned about the Claimant's performance and instructed consultants to conduct surveillance of her movements.

Miss Baker complained to an Employment Tribunal that the surveillance constituted harassment on the grounds of disability. Although the Employment Tribunal found in favour of the Claimant, it acknowledged that it had not been asked to determine the question of disability. The EAT, on appeal, confirmed that the protection of the discrimination legislation was not available to those who merely asserted a disability. It must be proven that the individual in question actually has a disability, are associated with a disabled person, or are wrongly perceived to be a disabled person.

Age discrimination in the workplace

On 1st October 2006, The Employment Equality (Age) Regulations (EE(A) Regs) took effect, outlawing age discrimination in both the workplace and vocational training. These Regulations have now been replaced wholesale by the Equality Act 2010. It is against the law to treat a person unfairly at work because of age. It is against the law to discriminate for being too young or old. The law only covers work, adult education and training. The law applies to a person whether working or applying for a job. It is against the law to bully or make offensive comments in the workplace because of age.

There are some exceptions to the general rule. For example, an employer may occasionally be allowed to discriminate against someone because of their age but only if they can show that this is justified. An employer may argue that it doesn't make business sense to employ someone over 60 years of age if there is a long and involved period of training allied to the job.

There are several cases of note here. the first was the recent case of Gomes v Henworth Ltd, a Winkworth estate agency at the Watford EAT June 2017. A woman who was told she might be "better suited to a traditional estate agency" was discriminated against because of her age, the tribunal ruled. Ms Gomes, who was 59 when the comment was made, started working for Henworth, which traded as Winkworth Estate Agents, in February 2015 as an administrative assistant. She had worked for another agent in the Winkworth franchise since February 2009 before being transferred.

In February 2016, the company's lettings director had a meeting with Gomes to discuss her work, in which he told her she needed to be more careful with her work. This upset Gomes so she spoke to her line manager who, in turn, spoke to Graham Gold, one of the directors.

In March 2016, Gold asked Gomes to meet with him and told her: "This marriage isn't working." When she asked what this meant, Gold mentioned a letter had been typed and sent to a solicitor with errors, including referring to the solicitor as a deceased client's son and referring to the deceased as 'Mrs' rather than 'Mr', and a note would be placed on her performance record.

Gold then said she would be "better suited to a traditional estate agency", which Gomes claimed she took to mean he thought she was too old to work in that particular office.

Allowing Gomes' claim for age discrimination, the tribunal concluded the phrase 'better suited to a traditional estate agency' was a reference to her age, noting that it was defined in the Oxford English Dictionary as 'long established' and it was unlikely that such a comment would have been made to a younger employee. The tribunal also allowed the claims for harassment related to age and constructive unfair dismissal.

Another case of note, relating to sex discrimination and other factors was the long running case of BAE systems v Marion Konczak wghich ran from 2006 until it was decided in 2017 by the court of appeal.

Mrs Konczak was a secretary at BAE from 1998 until her dismissal in 2007. She experienced a series of stressful events. In April 2006, after a particularly difficult meeting, her line manager said that women take things more emotionally than men, who tend to forget things and move on. That comment, described in the judgment as the "Dent comment", was the final straw for Mrs Konczak, who did not return to work due to work-related stress.

The Employment Tribunal held that the Dent comment was an act of sex discrimination. It also upheld several other complaints, including of discriminatory dismissal in 2007, but the Dent comment was the important finding for the purposes of the Court of Appeal's decision. Following prolonged proceedings, in October

2014 the Employment Tribunal held that the Dent comment had caused Mrs Konczak's illness and that BAE was liable for all losses flowing from it, amounting to around £360,000. BAE argued on appeal that it was wrong in principle for it to be liable for such a large amount, especially given the various other events, for which it was not legally liable, which it said had contributed to Mrs Konczak's illness. It argued that the correct approach was for the tribunal to apportion liability between the different factors, following the decision of the EAT in *Thaine v London School of Economics* [2010] UKEAT 0144/10, [2010] ICR 1422. The Court of Appeal thought differently and BAE lost the case.

Retirement and age discrimination
The normal retirement age for both men and women is 65, unless the employment contract states that it is higher. An employer was allowed to force a person to retire at the normal retirement age.

However, with the scrapping of the Default Retirement Age between April and October 2011, employers are no longer be able to force employees to retire at 65.

Unfair dismissal
It is discriminatory to dismiss a person because of age. A claim for unfair dismissal may be made if this has been the case.

****

Chapter 4

Business law-Company Law

When people set up a business they will usually form a (limited) company or a partnership. The main distinction between a company and a partnership is that the company is treated as a separate entity, or person in law. The partnership, on the other hand is not seen as a separate entity and consists only of those who have chosen to join together for business purposes.

One other crucial distinction is that a company will pay corporation tax, whilst a partnership will pay only that tax due as an individual liability. A company has access to what is known as "limited liability". This is where the liability for debt of directors is limited. Not all companies are limited companies. If a company is not limited there is no requirement to file accounts at Companies House. Partnerships have no such access to limited liability.

A company can separate ownership from control. People who subscribe to a company and purchase its shares do not necessarily have any control over the company or a hand in running the business. This is especially the case in a large Public Limited Company, where shareholders receive a return on their investment in the company. A further distinction and advantage for a company is in the area of raising finance. The company as a separate entity can raise finance in its own right, mortgage any assets by way of a floating charge, and generally enjoy access to finance that is not available to a partnership.

Public companies and private companies

Another main area which runs through company law is that of the distinction between the public company and the private company.

The majority of companies in the United Kingdom are private companies. One main feature of company law is that, with a few exceptions, the same rules apply to private companies as to public companies.

The second EC directive on company law did, however, lead to modifications to company law, with distinctions being drawn between public and private companies, these being incorporated into the Companies Act 2006.

One main feature of a public company is that it must have a minimum subscribed share capital of at least £50,000, or its equivalent in Euros paid up to at least 25 percent before it can be incorporated (s586 of the CA 2006). The second EC directive sets out the regulations for this, with the minimum subscribed share capital for public companies within the EU being £25,000 ECU. In addition to the payment of the minimum subscribed share capital to at least 25 percent on initial allotment of shares, the whole of any premium must be paid up. A further distinction between public and private companies is in the name of the company. The Companies Act of 2006 states that a public company must end with suffix "public limited company" or the abbreviation PLC. In Wales the term is cwmni cyhoeddus cyfyngedig with the abbreviation ccc. A private company will end with the term "limited" or the Welsh equivalent cyfyngedig or "cyf".

In addition, another fundamental distinction between the public and private company is that the private company is prohibited from seeking finance from the public by offering shares or debentures. The public company is authorised to seek shares in this way.

It is worth noting that most public companies are not listed-as of January 2018 there were 6,271 public companies of which only 2,329 were listed. Listed companies have to comply with more and more regulations. Currently, in addition to complying with the companies Act 2006, listed companies are also required to comply with the provisions of Pt V1 of the Financial Services and Markets

Act 2000 and a body of rules collectively known as the Listing Regime, which principally consists of (i) The Disclosures and Transparency Rules (ii) the Prospectus Rules and most importantly (iii) The Listing Rules. These latter rules are drafted and administered by the Financial Conduct Authority and impose obligations upon listed companies in relation to the disclosure of information, as well as supplementing the CA 2006 as regards certain areas of internal control. These rules have the force of law as the FCA is regarded as the 'competent authority' under part V1 of the Financial Services and Markets Act 2000.

Company limited by guarantee

A company limited by guarantee is private company, very like a private company limited by shares, but it does not have a share capital. It is widely used for charities, clubs, community enterprises and some co-operatives. The vast majority of such companies are non-profit distributing, but they do not have to be.

A company limited by guarantee is registered at Companies House, has articles of association, directors, etc., and is subject to all the requirements of the Companies Acts (except those relating to shares). There are no shares and so no shareholders, but such a company does have members, who meet and control the company through general meetings. The directors are often called a management committee or council of management, etc. but in law are still company directors and subject to all the rules that affect other directors. A company limited by guarantee confers limited liability as effectively as a company limited by shares. The articles state that the members guarantee to pay its debts, but only up to a fixed amount each. Usually that sum is £1, and no member can be liable for more than that amount if the company fails. The Companies Act 2006 also outlines other distinctions between companies:

- A private company can operate with one director, in contrast to the public company which is required to have two

- A private company needs only to have one member whereas a public company has to have two (s154 CA 2006).

- The company secretary of a private company can be anyone and that person needs no particular qualifications. There is now no legal requirement for a company secretary of a private company under the CA 2006. The company secretary of a public company must be qualified, holding a recognised qualification in this area in order to hold the post.

- Before a public company can pay a dividend, it must ensure that it has trading profits and that its capital assets are maintained in value to at least the value of the subscribed share capital plus undistributable reserves. There is no such rule applying to a private company (CA 2006)

- Before a public company can distribute shares in exchange for property it must obtain an independent experts valuation of the property. This requirement does not apply to a private company (CA 2006)

- A public company may not issue shares in exchange for services. This rule does not apply to a private company (CA 2006).

- The Directors of a public company must call an Extraordinary General Meeting (EGM) if it suffers a serious loss of capital. There is no requirement for a private company to do this.

- Proxies in a private company may speak at a meeting. In a public company there is no such right.

- In a private company there are courses of action which may be taken in order to dispense with formalities such as the need to hold an Annual General Meeting, the laying of accounts and the annual appointment of auditors. This is not the case with a public company, which is rigidly bound.

- Private companies may act by unanimous written resolution, in most cases. This does not apply to public companies.
- Where there is a proposal to elect a director aged 70 or over to the board of a public company, special notice is required. There is no such requirement for a private company.
- The minimum age for a company director under the CA 2006 s57, for both private and public companies is 16.

Limited Liability Partnerships

Under the Limited Liability Partnerships Act 2000, it is possible to create a different form of business association called a limited liability partnership. Under the LLPA 2000, a LLP becomes a corporate body with a legal personality separate from that of its members. It follows therefore that members of a LLP will not normally become liable for the debts of the LLP. The law relating to ordinary partnerships does not relate to a LLP.

Many of the detailed provisions relating to LLP's are to be found in secondary legislation, in particular the Limited Partnership Regulations 2001. These regulations apply some of the provisions of the CA 2006 and the Insolvency Act 1986 to LLP's with some modifications to reflect the different nature of an LLP.

Formation of an LLP

An LLP is created by registration with the registrar of companies. Once the registrar has registered an LLP and issued a certificate of incorporation, a new corporate body with a separate legal personality of its own is created. Section 2 (1) of the LPA 2000 provides that:

Two or more persons associated for carrying on a lawful business with a view to profit must have subscribed their names to an incorporation document which is to be delivered to the registrar of companies.

Community Interest Companies

The Companies (Audit, Investigations and Community Enterprise) Act 2004 and regulations made under the Act, establish the legislative framework for CICs. CICs are regulated by the CIC Regulator.

A Community Interest Company can be registered in England and Wales, Scotland or Northern Ireland. It is a hybrid between a charity and a profit making company. A Community Interest Company must be set up and run for the benefit of the community. A CIC can only be registered with the consent of the Community Interest Companies Regulator. The application must comply with CIC legislation as well as the usual rules for registration of a company. The CIC Regulator has to be satisfied that the proposed company is being set up to benefit the community and that its articles include all the provisions required of a community interest company. Each year, the CIC must submit a return stating what its activities have been and that these have been of community benefit.

Property management companies

A property management company in England and Wales, Scotland or Northern Ireland is a particular type of company: one set up to hold an interest in a property which is divided into units, each unit being owned separately. A typical example is a large house which has been divided into a number of flats (sometimes called a flat management company), each flat being owned by one or two people. Such a company can also be used for large blocks of flats, housing estates and commercial properties divided into units. A property management company will always be a private limited company. It may be limited by shares or limited by guarantee. People who deal with property management companies professionally tend to have their preferences. It is one of those circumstances where either type of company will work perfectly well. The only significant difference between them is that a company limited by shares has a share capital, owned by its shareholders and a company limited by guarantee does not, but is controlled by its shareholders. If the company is to own the freehold, some people prefer it to be a company limited by shares as this gives a form of ownership between the shareholders (who own the company) and the property (which is owned by the company). On the other hand, with a company limited by guarantee, there is no need to transfer a share when the flat is sold.

The concept of the corporate personality

The principle of the separate legal personality of a company was established in an important case, Saloman v A Saloman (1897). The facts of the case were that Saloman had incorporated his shoe repair business, transferring it to a company. He took all the shares of the company with the exception of six which were held by his wife, daughter and four sons. Part of the payment for transfer of the business was made in the form of debentures (secured loan) issued by the company to Saloman. Saloman transferred the debentures to Broderip in exchange for a loan. Saloman defaulted on payment of interest on the loan and Broderip sought to enforce the security against the company. Unsecured creditors tried to put the company into liquidation. There was a dispute between Broderip and the unsecured creditors over who had priority over payment of the debt. It was argued for the creditors that Salmons security was void as the company was a sham and was in reality the agent of Salomon.

The House of Lords held that this was not the case as the company had been properly incorporated and therefore the security was valid and could be enforced. This case is seen as one of the most important cases in company law as it is from this that many principles of company law flow. There are certain statutory exceptions to the Salmon principle and they are as follows:

- Section 7 of the Companies Act 2006 provides that if the membership of a public company falls below the statutory minimum of two then the remaining member should after a period of six months grace, be liable for the company's debts and obligations where he or she knew of the situation.

- Section 767 (3) of the Companies Act 2006 provides that where a public company fails to obtain a trading certificate in addition to its certificate of incorporation before trading and borrowing money then the companies directors are liable for any obligations incurred.

- Sections 398-408 of the Companies Act 2006 provides that where a group situation exists (i.e. where there is a holding company and subsidiaries) then group accounts should be prepared. In assessing whether this is the case, clearly the veil is being lifted to see if the holding company/subsidiary relationship exists.

- Section 83 of the Companies Act 2006 provides that if a company officer misdescribes the company in a letter, bill, invoice, order, receipt or any other document then the officer is liable in the event of the obligation not being honored.

- Section 994 of the Companies Act 2006 may involve lifting the veil to determine, for example, the basis on which the company was formed.

- Sections 1159-1160 of the Companies Act 2006 set out the formula for determining if a holding company/subsidiary company relationship exists.

- Section 15 of the Company Directors Disqualification Act 1986 provides that if a director who is disqualified continues to act, he or she will be personally liable for the debts and obligations of the company.

- Section 122 (1) (g) of the Insolvency Act 1986 provides that a petitioner may present a petition to wind up a company on the just and equitable ground.

- On occasion, this may be based on a situation involving the lifting of the company veil in order to determine the basis of the company formation.

- Section 213 of the Insolvency Act 1986 provides that where a person trades through the medium of a company, knowing that the company is unable to pay its debts, he or she may be held liable for contributions to the companies assets where the company is being wound up. This has a criminal counterpart in s999 (1) of the CA 2006.

- Section 6 of the Law of Property Act 1969 provides that where a person has a controlling interest in a company which is carrying on a business, the business is treated as the controller for the purposes of refusing a renewal of a tenancy issued out of the Landlord and Tenant Act 1954.

In addition to the statutory exceptions to the Salomon principle there are certain judicial decisions which have had an impact. One such decision is that of combating fraud. There are several well-known legal cases that have dealt with fraud.

One such case is that of Jones v Lipman (1962) where a vendor decided to sell a piece of land and then changed his mind. This resulted in the would-be purchaser suing for specific performance. In order to avoid this, the vendor transferred the piece of land to a company. The courts held that although the company was another legal entity nevertheless the action was designed to avoid legal action and the courts refused to accept the action of transferring the land and ordered specific performance against the vendor.

Therefore the action of transferring assets from the individual to a company in order to change a legal status is not tolerated if it is seen as fraudulent, as in the case above. There are numerous other examples of a company veil being lifted in order to combat fraud.

Group structures

Group structures are governed by s1159 of the CA 2006. Sometimes the fact that a company is within a group is seen as a reason for identifying it with another company within the group. In Harold Holdsworth and Co (Wakefield) Ltd v Caddies (1955) the respondent held an employment contract with the appellant company to serve it as managing director. The House of Lords held that the appellant company could require the respondent to serve a subsidiary company.

A fundamental case in this area is DHN Food Distributors Ltd v Tower Hamlets London Borough Council (1976). This case concerned compensation for compulsory purchase. The company operating the business was the holding company and the premises were owned by the companies wholly owned subsidiary. Compensation was only payable for disturbance to the companies business if the business was operated on land owned by the company. In this case, Lord Denning said:

"In many respects a group of companies are treated together for the purposes of accounts, they are treated as one concern. This is especially the case when a parent company owns all the shares of the subsidiary-so much so that it can control the activities of the subsidiaries. These subsidiaries are bound hand and foot and must do just what the parent company says."

Companies and crimes and negligence

Companies, as any individual, can commit crimes, although there are certain obvious exceptions, such as rape or murder. A company can, however, commit manslaughter. In December 1994, OLL Limited became the first company in England to be convicted of manslaughter. This arose from the death of four young people in a canoeing accident in Lyme Bay which was organised by the company. In the case, Kite v OLL Ltd the managing director of the company that organised the trip was imprisoned for manslaughter and the company fined £60,000.

The Law Commission reported on the law of corporate manslaughter in consultation paper no 135 (1994). They recommended a new offence based on whether the companies conduct fell significantly below what could reasonably be expected of it in the context of the significant risk of death or injury of which it should have been aware. In a later report (Law Commission Paper no 237) Legislating the Criminal Code, Involuntary Manslaughter (1996) the Law Commission, in its final report, called for a new offence of corporate killing comparable to killing by gross negligence. It is imperative that at least one person should be recognised and identified as the directing force of the company causing death by gross negligence when acting as the company.

In the only other case of a company being convicted of manslaughter, Jackson Transport (Ossett) Ltd. The company concerned was a medium sized company employing about 40 people. A person was killed in May 1994 while he was cleaning behind a tanker containing chemicals. Mr. Jackson, the owner, ran the business himself and he and the company was convicted of manslaughter. Companies may also commit strict liability offences. This is important in areas such as pollution and food safety. There is however, a diligence defence and if the company can demonstrate the practice of diligence, or that lack of diligence was on the part of a person who was not the true embodiment of the company, it will escape liability.

****

4. 2

The Constitution of a Company

Under the Companies Act 2006, the importance of a company's memorandum of association has been reduced to a mere historical record. Constitutional provisions are to be contained within the Articles of Association instead. The memorandum is a document that needs to be submitted as part of the incorporation process and will not be capable of amendment. The information that was contained within the memorandum will now be provided to the registrar in an application for registration under s 9 of the Companies Act 2006. The application for registration must contain the following::

- The name of the company (s9) (2) of the Companies Act 2006.
- If the company is a public company a statement indicating this
- s 9(2).
- A statement that the registered office of the company is situated in England and Wales, in Wales or in Scotland s9 (7).

The application must also contain:

- A statement of initial shareholding
- A Statement of share capital
- A Statement of guarantee
- A Statement of proposed officers
  - A Statement of compliance

Objects clauses and *ultra vires*

By virtue of s 31 of the CA 2006 unless a company's articles specifically restrict the objects of the company, its objects are unrestricted. If the company does decide to amend its objects, then this change must be made by amendment to the articles. The new law is stated in s 40 of the CA 2006. The effect of the new law is to effectively abolish *ultra vires*. However, there are still occasions where a challenge could arise. These are where a director or connected person is involved or a third party acted in bad faith. A Challenge could also arise if an injunction is sought to prevent directors acting or to allege a breach of duty after events. S 239 of the CA 2006 now only requires ordinary resolutions to ratify any breaches of duty by directors. However, the votes of any director or person involved in the breach of duty will not count. S 41 (3) of the CA 2006 makes any directors involved liable to account for the transaction and to indemnify the company whether they knew they were exceeding their powers or not.

The position at common law
The old case will still be applicable in certain limited circumstances. Prior to statutory reform, at common law, contracts that were outside the scope of the company's objects were held to be *ultra vires* and void.

Before statutory intervention therefore the question was simple: if the objects clause covered the relevant contract it was valid. If it was outside the scope of the company's permitted range of activities it was void and unenforceable. There are several cases which serve to highlight the nature of the above. One such case is that of Payne and Co Ltd (1904) where a company borrowed money which was then used for purposes outside of the objects of the company. The lender was able to enforce the loan because he did not know the purpose of the loan. In Re John Beauforte Ltd (1953) a different decision was reached on the basis that a supplier to the company provided coke. The company could have been using the coke for internal purposes as it was engaged in the manufacturer of veneered panels. The order was placed on notepaper showing that the company was engaged in this business and the courts held that the combination of constructive notice of what the company could do and the actual notice of what it was doing was fatal to the suppliers claim.

Statutory intervention

Article 9 of the first EC directive on company law provided as follows:

- Acts done by the organs of the company shall be binding upon it even if those acts are not within the objects of the company, unless such acts exceed powers that the law confers or allows to be conferred on those organs.
- Since that first article, company law has developed and now the Companies Act 2006 has amended the law on ultra vires and objects clauses.
- The Prentice Report (reform of the ultra vires rule, a consultative document (1986) (par 50) put forward the following recommendations in relation to the reform of the ultra vires rule:
- A company should have the capacity to do any act whatsoever
- A third party dealing with the company should not be affected by the contents of any document merely because it is registered with the registrar of companies or with the company.
- A company should be bound by the acts of its board or an individual director.
- The third party should be under no obligation to determine the scope of the authority of a company's board or individual director, or the contents of the company's articles or memorandum.
- A third party who has actual knowledge that a board or an individual director do not possess the authority to enter into a transaction on behalf of the company should not be allowed to enforce against the company but the company should be free to ratify this. The same result should obtain where a third party has knowledge that the transaction falls outside of the

company's objects, but in this case ratification should be by a special resolution.

- Knowledge in this context will require understanding, and it will only be the knowledge of the individual entering into the particular transaction that will be relevant
- The proposal (in relation to third parties) should be modified where a third party is an officer or director of the company and in this situation constructive knowledge should be sufficient to render the transaction unenforceable and for this purpose constructive knowledge should mean the type of knowledge which may reasonably be expected of a person carrying out the functions of that director or officer of the company.
- In consequence of the recommendations of the Prentice Report the Companies Act of 1989 amended the law on ultra vires and objects clauses.

The Companies act of 2006, provides that the validity of an act done by a company shall not be called into question on the ground of lack of capacity by reason of anything in the company's memorandum. A transaction can thus be enforced by an outsider or the company.

A member may, however, restrain the company from entering into a transaction which is outside the company's objects. This power to restrain the company can only operate where the company has not entered into a binding transaction to perform the act.

If the directors exceed limitations on their powers then they are in breach of their director's duties. Even if the directors conclude a contract outside of the objects clause, and a member has not succeeded in restraining this, the company may be able to sue their directors for breach of duties (Companies Act 2006). It is open to the company to ratify what has been done by special resolution. The company may also ratify by a separate special resolution the breach of the director's duties thereby putting the matter outside of litigation.

S.40 (1) of the CA now provides that where a person deals with a company in good faith the power of the directors to bind the company shall be deemed to be free of any limitation under the company's constitution. The outsider is not to be regarded as in bad faith by reason only by his knowing that the transaction was outside of the director's powers.

Further, this section provides that:
...a party to any transaction with a company is not bound to enquire as to whether it is permitted by the companies memorandum or as to any limitations on the board of directors to bind the company or to authorise others to do so.

The wording under sections s.40 (1) will protect outsiders in most circumstances. The CA 2006 builds on these provisions, which extends to other officers acting on behalf of the company.

This provides that:
... a person shall not be taken to have notice of any such matters merely because of its being disclosed in any document kept by the registrar of companies (and thus available for inspection) or made available by the company for inspection.

The rules governing company names
The first clause in the company's memorandum should be the name of that company. The statutory provisions relating to company names are set out in The Companies Act 2006. These provisions are as follows:

- Section 58 of the CA 2006 provides that the name of a public company must end with the word "PLC" or the Welsh equivalent as mentioned. A private company limited by shares or guarantee should end with "Limited" or the abbreviation Ltd or the Welsh equivalent as mentioned.

- In certain cases, a private limited company may be permitted to omit the word "limited" from the end of its name. The Companies Act 2006 permits companies to omit the word limited on satisfying certain conditions. The company concerned must be a private limited company and have as its objects the promotion of science, commerce, art, education, religion, charity or any profession and anything incidental or conductive to any of these objects and must have a requirement in its constitution that its profits or other income be applied in promoting these objects. The constitution must also prohibit the payment of dividends to its members and require all of the assets which would otherwise be available to its members generally to be transferred on its winding up to another body with similar objects or to a body the objects of which are the promotion of charity and anything incidental.
- Section 53 of the Companies Act 2006 prohibits the use of certain names. The words public limited company, limited and unlimited can only be used at the end of a company name as may be the Welsh equivalents.
- The name must not be the same as a name already registered at Companies House. (s 66 CA 2006)
- S 55 of the CA 2006 states that there are certain words and expressions, which require the prior permission of either the Secretary for State or some other designated body.. There is a list of the words specified in regulations made under s55 of the Companies Act. If the name of the company implies some regional, national or international pre-eminence, governmental link or sponsorship or some pre-eminent status, then consent may be required.
- The choice of company name is limited by other considerations. If the name is a registered trademark the person who owns the trademark may take action to prevent the use of the name under the Trades Mark Act 1994.

- The use of a name which is already used by an existing business (whether sole trader, partnership or company) or a name which is similar to that of an existing business such that it appears to the public that there is a link between the two businesses may be subject to legal action, such as an injunction to restrain the company from further use.

Change of name

Section 77 (1) of the Companies Act 2006 provides that a company may change its name by special resolution in general meeting.

There are other provisions relating to change of name, that is if the Secretary of State or Companies House gives a direction that the company must do this. This will usually happen in a situation where the original name was misleading or that the name itself is deemed to be of potential harm.

The articles of association of a company

The articles of association is now the most important document to be submitted to the registrar (CA 2006 s 18). the articles tend to regulate the internal workings of the company and typically cover such issues as the balance of power between the members and the directors, the conduct of general meetings, and certain issues pertaining to shares and distribution of assets.

Although a company must have articles of association, the contents of the articles are not laid down by the 2006 CA. Under s 20 of the 2006 CA, a limited company doesn't have to register articles. If they are not registered then model articles drafted under the Companies (Model Articles) Regulations can be adopted. Section 21 of the Companies Act 2006 allows a company to alter its articles by special resolution. However, the power to alter the articles of a company is restricted by the following:

- The company cannot alter its articles in a way which would lead to contravention of the 2006 Companies Act.
- Any alteration of the company's articles which would lead to a difference between, or a clash between the memorandum is void.
- If an alteration of the articles is proposed which conflicts with an order of the court then this would be automatically void.
- If the proposed alteration of the articles leads to an alteration of the class rights then special procedures need to be followed in addition to a special resolution being passed. A company must follow a regime which is appropriate to the variation of class rights which is set out in s121 of the 2006 Companies Act.

If a change of articles involves a variation of class rights then this procedure must be followed. If a company has more than one class of shares then questions of variations of class rights sometimes arise. Once it has been determined that there is more than one class of share in the company then the next question for determination is whether there has been a variation of rights attached to those shares. Once it has been established that there has been a variation of class rights then the rules that have to be followed to carry the variation into effect are dependent upon whether the company has a share capital or not. If the company has a share capital then the rights may be varied:

    a) in accordance with provision in the company's articles for the variation of those rights; or

    b) where the company's articles contain no such provision, if the members of that class consent to the variation in accordance with this section.

    c) The consent required for the purposes of this section on the part of the members of a class is-

d) consent in writing from at least three quarters of the members of the class, or

e) a special resolution passed at a separate general meeting of the members of that class sanctioning the variation.

If class rights are varied, dissentient minorities have special rights to object to the alteration. They must satisfy certain conditions. The dissenters must hold no less than 15% of the issued shares of the class and must not have voted in favour of the resolution (s 633 of the CA 2006). They may then object to the variation within 21 days of consent being given to the resolution.

If the class rights are varied under a procedure set out in the memorandum or articles of association of the company or if the class rights are set out otherwise than in the memorandum or articles are silent on variation, then dissentient minorities have special rights to object to the alteration. They must satisfy certain conditions:

• The dissenters must hold no less than 15 percent of the issued shares of the class and must not have voted in favour of the resolution. They may then object to the variation within 21 days of the consent being given to the resolution. On occasions, their objections may be upheld by the courts (s 623 CA 2006).

'Bona Fide for the benefit of the company as a whole'

In addition to the various statutory restrictions considered above, the power to alter a company's articles is subject to the overriding principle that any alteration must be bona fide for the benefit of the company as a whole. One case that illustrates this is Allen v Gold Reefs of West Africa Limited (1900). In this case, the company's articles originally provided:

.....that the company shall have a first and paramount lien for all debts obligations and liabilities of any member to and towards the company upon all shares (not being fully paid) held by such member..........

The alteration proposed was to delete the words 'not being fully paid' to provide the company with a lien over any shares of a member where a debt was due from that member. The alteration was challenged. Lindley MR said as follows:

Wide, however, as the language of s 50 is (now section 21 of the CA 2006) the power conferred by it must, like all other powers, be exercised subject to those general principles of law and equity which are applicable to all powers conferred on majorities and enabling them to bind minorities stock. It must be exercised not only in the manner required by the law, but also bona fide for the benefit of the company as a whole, and it must not be exceeded. These conditions are always implied and are seldom, if ever, expressed. But, if they are complied with, I can discover no grounds for judicially putting other restrictions on the power conferred by the section and those contained within it.

In the instant case the Court of Appeal held that the power had been exercised *bona fide*.

The constitution as a contract

The courts have long held that a companies articles form a contract between a company and its members, and between the members themselves as in the case Tavarone Mining Co (Pritchards Case) 1873. Section 33(1) of the CA 2006 expands upon this by stating that:

The provisions of a company's constitution binds the company and its members to the same extent as if they were covenants on the part of the company and of each member to observe those provisions. Accordingly, the company's constitution forms what is known as the 'statutory contract' and imposes obligations upon:

• the company when dealing with its members

- the members when dealing with the company
- the members when dealing with each other.

The statutory contract

the statutory contract created by s33 is unusual in that differs from a standard contract and is not subject to standard contractual rules. One cardinal rules that does apply to the statutory contract is the doctrine of privity of contract The stautory contract is formed between a company and its members-persons not party to the contract are therefore not permitted to enforce the rules of the constitution. One case that demonstrates this is Eley v Positive Government Security Life Assurance Co (1876) where Eley, a solicitor drafted the defendant company articles, which were then registered. the articles provided that Eley would act as the company solicitor and could not be removed unless guilty of misconduct. Soon after, the company ceased to employ Eley and employed another solicitor and Eley alleged that the company had breached the terms of contract. Eley lost the case as Eley was not party to the statutory contract and therefore could not sue.

The contract between the company and its members

As the constitution forms a contract between the company and its members, it follows that both parties can enforce compliance with the terms of the constitution against the other. In the case of Hickman v Kent or Romney Marsh Sheepbreeders Association (1915) the company's articles provided that any dispute between it and a member should be referred for arbitration before any legal proceedings were initiated. The company purported to expel one of its members (Hickman) from its organisation but, instead of referring the dispute to arbitration, Hickman petitioned the High Court for an injunction restraining his expulsion.

It was held that the articles formed a contract between the company and its members. The company was therefore permitted to enforce the term of the articles and require disputes to be referred to arbitration. the High Court stayed Hickmans legal proceedings and he was subsequently expelled.

Member enforcing compliance of a term of the constitution

A member can enforce compliance of a term of the constitution against the company, as occurred in the case of Pender v Lushington (1877) where the company's articles provided that its members would have one vote for every ten shares up to a maximum of 100 votes. Consequently, members with over 1,000 shares would not have voting power commensurate to their shares. To avoid this, members with over 1,000 shares (of which Pender was one) transferred some of their excess shares to several nominees, thereby unlocking the votes within them. the company's chairman (Lushington) refused to accept the nominees votes and Pender alleged that his votes were improperly rejected. Penders action succeeded The shares were properly transferred and registered to nominees so refusing to accept their votes constituted a breach of the articles.

It is important to note that not all the terms of the constitution can be enforced this way. As Buckley LJ stated in Blagood v Henderson's Transvaal Estates Ltd (1908) , 'the purpose of the constitution is to define the position of the shareholder as shareholder and not to bind him in his capacity as an individual'.

The contract between members themselves

Just as the constitution forms a contract between the company and its members , so too does it form a contract amongst the members themselves. Accordingly, a breach of the statutory contract by a member can be enforced by another member, providing that the provision breached concerns a members rights.

In the case Rayfield v hands (1960) the company's articles provided that, if a member wished to sell his shares, he should inform the directors, who would then purchase the shares between them.   Rayfield wished to sell his shares and so notified the directors, but the directors refused to purchase his shares. the directors were all members of the company, and so Rayfield sought an order requiring the directors to purchase his shares. The court ordered that the directors should purchase Rayfields shares. As the company was a quasi partnership, the article provision affected the directors in their capacity as members. Accordingly, the provision concerned a membership right and formed part of the statutory contract.

The capacity of a company

As the company is a legal person, it can enter into contracts in much the same way as natural persons can. However, historically, the company's ability to enter into contracts was subject to a significant limitation. prior to the passing of the CA 2006, all companies were required to state in their memoranda the objects or purposes for which the company was set up (this is known as the 'objects clause') the objects clause serves to limit the contractual capacity of the company and if a company entered into a contract that was outside the scope of its objects clause, the company would be acting *ultra vires* (beyond ones powers) and the contract would be void.   This restriction on a company's capacity was introduced to protect a person who provided a company with capital, namely members and creditors. Such persons provided capital on the expectation that the company would pursue lines of business for which it was set up and not for activities outside of the company's remit.

The abolition of the requirement to include an objects clause

the requirement of an objects clause has been abolished by the CA 2006 (although companies can still include an objects clause if they wish and such companies will accordingly have unrestricted objects (CA 2006 s 31.(1). For those companies incorporated before the passing of the CA 2006 a special resolution by company members can delete existing objects clauses, thereby acquiring unrestricted capacity

Alteration of the articles

As a company, or the markets that it operates in evolves , it may be necessary for it to alter its articles. Section 21 (1) of the CA 2006 provides that a company may amend its articles by passing a special resolution and, in certain cases, the courts also have the power to amend the articles. However, it should be noted that the ability to alter the articles is not limitless and both statute and common law impose restrictions on a company's ability to alter its articles.

Entrenched article provisions

A company cannot make its articles unalterable (Walker v London Tramways co (1879). However, the CA 2006 s.22 introduced the ability to entrench company article provisions, making it more difficult to alter. This could be done by requiring additional conditions to be met.

In order to prevent abuse the Act imposes several safeguards, including:

- Entrenchment will not prevent alteration where all of the members agree to an alteration, or where the court orders an alteration to be made.
- If a company wishes to entrench an article provision after the company has been formed, it can only do so with the agreement of all the members of the company.

****

4.3

Company Finance

___

The role and definition of the promoter

Although there is no statutory definition of a promoter, case law has developed as definition. In the case Twycross v Grant (1877) a promoter is defined as "one who undertakes to form a company with reference to a given project and to set it going, and who takes the necessary steps to accomplish that purpose."

In Emma silver Mining Co v Grant (1879) Lord Lindley stated that the term had no very definite meaning. Whether or not a person is a promoter is a question of fact. Promoters are quite often a company's first directors. The importance of establishing whether a person is a promoter lies partly in locating liability for acts done on behalf of or in connection with the company to be formed, for example, for statements in prospectuses. Not yet being in existence, the company cannot be liable. Promoters are not necessarily partners with each other (Keith Spicer and Mansell (1970)). Mainly it rests in deciding whether a person owes promoters fiduciary duty to the company.

Liability of a promoter

A promoter may become liable to third parties for misrepresentation or perhaps as the partner of another promoter under agency principles in partnership law. The traditional area of liability to the company is for breach of the fiduciary duties he owes it during his time of promotion.

Equity will not allow the promoter to taking advantage of his privileged position in relation to the unborn company. He must make full disclosure to it, when formed, of his interest in any transaction and must not profit from his position without the company's free consent. Otherwise, he must account personally for profits made and hold on constructive trust any property received which came to him by virtue of being a promoter.

A promoter must disclose fully the extent and the nature of his interest and profit. The duty cannot be avoided by setting up a company with a board of directors which cannot, and does not "exercise an independent and intelligent judgment on the transaction" and disclosing merely to that board.

In Erlanger v New Sombrero (1878) a syndicate headed by Erlanger, a French banker, acquired for £55,000 a lease of an island in the West Indies with phosphate mining rights. Erlanger then arranged for the syndicate to set up a company and to appoint its first directors, who were in reality puppets. The lease was sold, through a first party nominee, to the new company for £110,000 and within days of the company being established, the sale and purchase were ratified by the directors. The full details were not disclosed to members of the public who became shareholders. After the initial phosphate shipments proved unsuccessful, the true circumstances were revealed and the shareholders replaced the board of directors. It was held that the sale of the lease should be rescinded, the lease to be returned to the syndicate, which had to repay the purchase price to the company. The directors should not contribute to disadvantaging the shareholders. Disclosure to the members would be effective if they acquiesced (Lagunas Nitrate v Lagunas Syndicate (1899) but not if an undue advantage over investors remained e.g. if the original members comprised or were otherwise under the influence of the promoters (Gluckstein v Barnes) (1990).

Remedies

The company may be able to rescind contracts entered into consequent upon non-disclosure or misrepresentation by a promoter unless one of the bars to rescission has become operative i.e. affirmation (unless this amounts to ratification of breach of duty by way of fraud on the minority: Atwool v Merryweather (1867); lapse of time; intervening third party rights; inability to make restitutio in integrum; and the courts discretion to award damages in lieu of rescission (Misrepresentation Act 1967 s2 (2)).

Breach of fiduciary duty may result in liability to account and/or imposition of a constructive trust. But promoters should be able to retain expenses incurred in acquiring property in such cases (Bagnall v Carlton (1877)).

Remuneration and expenses

The promoter does his work and incurs expenses by the nature of his position, at a time before the company has become legally capable of acting. The company cannot therefore enter into a binding contract with him to pay him, nor can the company when formed validly ratify such an agreement made when it did not exist (retrospectively validate).

It cannot enter into a new contract after formation (except under seal) for the consideration he provides will be past.

The practical solution is for promoters to secure the insertion in the articles of a provision enabling the directors to pay promoter's expenses plus reasonable remuneration, which provision will be valid if full disclosure is made.

Pre–incorporation contracts

Similar difficulties arise with contracts purporting to be made between the company and third parties before incorporation. The company will not normally be bound by preliminary contracts. Nor will the promoter be liable for breach of implied warranty of authority if no implication can be made, the third party knowing the true facts. The company may be liable apart from contract, to pay a reasonable amount for benefits actually received, or for conversion, for refusing to permit the third party to retake goods delivered.

Rather than attempt to bind a company, a promoter might contract personally with a third party and forward benefits received to the company when formed, under a separate contract, subject to full disclosure. He might make the company liable on his original contract by assignment. Under The Companies Act 2006 s 21:

"A contract that purports to be made by or on behalf of a company at a time when the company has not been formed, has effect, subject to any agreement to the contrary, as one made with the person purporting to act for the company or as an agent for it, and he is personally liable on the contract accordingly."

The company's agent will be personally liable whether he purports to act on behalf of the company or signs the contract in the company's name alone, and he may be personally liable as both parties know the company is about to be formed and is not yet at the stage of being formed (Phonogram v Lane (1981). However, a person carrying out the affairs of an existing company under a new name which has not yet been registered will not be personally liable. Such a company is not one which has not been formed (Oshkosh B'Gosh v Dan Marbel (1988).

Trading certificate

A public company initially registered as such cannot commence business until the registrar receives a declaration that the nominal value of the allotted share capital meets the authorised minimum and, satisfied that it is, issues a trading certificate, (Companies Act 2006). This provision can be avoided by registering as a private company and registering as a public one.

Rules relating to payment for shares

The following matters should be checked where shares are to be issued by a public or private company:

- Does the company have sufficient authorized share capital for the issue?

- This may be checked by looking at the company's memorandum. If necessary, the authorized capital may be increased.

- Do the directors have authority to allot the shares? See s. 549 of the CA 2006. However, a private company may pass an elective resolution that s. 549 is not to apply to that company, since, normally, authority under s.551 of the CA 2006 can only last for a maximum period of five years, unless renewed.

- Do pre-emption rights apply? Section 561 of the CA 2006 makes statutory provision for pre-emption on second and subsequent issues of shares. This may be excluded by a private company in its constitution. It may be excluded by both private and public companies by special resolution.

The rules for payment for shares are based upon the Second EC Directive on company law. They are incorporated into the CA 2006. Section 582 (1) of the CA 2006 requires that shares should be paid up in money or money's worth. Section 582 (1) of the CA 2006 provides that a public company cannot accept an undertaking from a person to do work or perform services for shares. Section 580 of the CA 2006 requires that shares cannot be issued at a discount. This applies to both public and private companies. There are, however, exceptions to this principle:

- Shares may be issued to underwriters at a discount of up to 10 per cent (s. 553 of the CA 2006)

- Shares may be issued in exchange for services that happen to be overvalued in a private company. Shares may not be issued in exchange for services in a public company.

- Shares may be issued in exchange for property which is overvalued in a private company. In a public company, there is a need for an independent expert valuation of the property concerned (s. 593 CA 2006).

In a public company shares must be paid up at least one quarter of their nominal value plus the whole of any premium (CA 2006 s 586)

A public company cannot issue shares in exchange for a non cash consideration which may be transferred more than five years from the date of allotment (s. 587 (1) CA 2006). Where shares are issued at a premium (that is above their nominal value) in either a public or private company, the whole of the premium is placed in a share premium account. This is treated as if it were ordinary share capital for most purposes. It cannot be used to pay up a dividend. However, it may be used to pay up a bonus issue of shares (s. 610 CA 2006).

Small Business, Enterprise and Employment Act 2015: abolition of bearer shares

The Small Business, Enterprise and Employment Act 2015 received Royal Assent at the end of the last Parliament. The fuller implications will be discussed in chapter 4. The changes to bearer shares came into force in May 2015.

The key provisions

From 26 May 2015, the issue of new share warrants to bearer (also known as bearer shares) is not permitted. 26 May 2015 was the "commencement date" in a strict nine month timetable during which the holders of bearer shares had the right to surrender the warrants for conversion into registered shares. Companies with bearer shares in issue must have given various notices to the holders (including putting notices in the Gazette) informing them of their right to convert the bearer shares and the consequences of not doing so. The first notice must have been given within the period of one month following the commencement date.

Companies are be obliged to apply to court to cancel bearer shares if they were not surrendered for conversion within the surrender period and pay into court the amount of share capital (nominal and premium) paid up on the bearer shares to be cancelled, plus any accrued dividends.

Implications

Although bearer shares are not often used in UK companies now, they have been used historically, for example, for structuring and tax planning. Companies should contact holders of bearer shares now so that the shares can be converted, avoiding the need to apply to court for the cancellation of unconverted bearer shares and having to fund the payment into court of the amount of share capital to be cancelled. Public companies with bearer shares should pay particular attention to the amount of share capital attributable to the bearer shares because any cancellation of bearer shares which results in the share capital dropping below the minimum required by the Companies Act 2006, may force the company to re-register as a private company.

There are criminal sanctions for both the company and its officers for default in complying with the provisions. Holders of warrants who do not surrender their bearer shares for conversion within the nine month surrender period will lose their shares. Monies paid into court can be claimed for up to three years following cancellation, but only where the failure to exercise the right of surrender was due to "exceptional circumstances". Unclaimed monies will go to the Government.

The supervision and control of investments

The Financial Services Act 1986, as amended by the Financial Services and Markets Act 2000, provides for a regime to protect investors. The Act provides statutory regulation and self-regulation by the market. Deposit taking businesses are regulated by the Banking Act 1987.

The Financial Services Act, as amended, gives certain functions to the Secretary of State but also authorises that person to transfer such functions as felt appropriate to a designated agency. This has been done in the first place to the Securities and Investment Board (S.I.B.) a body formed and supported mainly by the financial services industry. Those who carry on an investment business must be "authorised persons" of whom a register is kept (FSA 1986 s102) or "exempted persons". (FSA 1986 s3). Otherwise they commit an offence and all transactions are unenforceable. Authorisation may be made by membership of a recognised professional body (FSA 1986 ss15-21) or by the Secretary of State (FSA 1986 s25). The commercial method is by membership of a recognised self-regulating organisation such as the Financial Intermediaries, Managers and Brokers Regulatory Association (FIMBRA). Exempted persons include: The Bank of England, clearing houses, Recognised Investment Exchanges such as the Stock Exchange and listed market institutions.

Except in the case of SRO's the Secretary of State is empowered to issue statements of principle and codes of practice regarding the conduct and financial standing expected of person authorised to carry on investment business (FSA 1986 ss57-58) and to make rules regulating the conduct of investment business by authorised persons for indemnification against civil liability incurred by authorised persons and for establishing a fund to compensate investors unable to obtain satisfaction of claims from authorised persons (FSA 1986 s54) and regulations with respect to money held by authorised persons (FSA 1986 s55).

The conduct of investment business
Subject to certain exceptions, the issue by or approval of an authorised person is necessary for the issue of an investment advertisment, which is an advertisement inviting people to enter into an investment agreement (FSA 1986 ss57-58). An investment agreement is one Involving dealing or advising on investments,

though not involving employee share schemes, sales of shares in private companies carrying over 75 percent of voting rights or where the terms of the transaction are uniform for all such transactions in the investment (FSA 1986 ss44(9) 20791) Sched 1). It is an offence knowingly or recklessly to make a misleading statement and to induce another to enter into, decline or refrain from exercising rights under an investment agreement, and without reasonably believing that he would not be so, to be involved in conduct creating a false impression as to the markets regarding investments and inducing a person to deal or refrain from dealing in those investments (FSA 1986 s 47).

On the Secretary of States application, the court may issue an injunction to prevent contravention of these provisions and order restitution of benefits (FSA 1986 s61).

The Securities market

For securities listed, or to be listed on the Stock Exchange it is necessary to comply with the requirements of the Financial Services Act 1986 part 1V. It empowers the Council of the Stock Exchange to make rules for this purpose, (FSA 1986 s142-144) including provisions for rectification for non-compliance with the rules. These rules on Admission of Securities to Listing (The Yellow Book) contain continuing disclosure requirements. Additionally to information required by the yellow book, the submitted listing particulars must contain such information as investors and their advisors would reasonably expect to make an informed assessment of the present and anticipated future rights and financial status of the securities (FSA 1986 ss146-148) and copies must be delivered to the registrar. Where listing particulars are to be published in connection with an application for listing, no other advertisement should be issued without the approval of the Stock Exchange (FSA 1896 s154).

A person acquiring relevant securities is entitled to be compensated by persons responsible for misleading particulars for loss suffered by reliance on the information unless they reasonably believed the statements or any detail were properly omitted (FSA 1986 ss150-152), but shareholders have no right to challenge cancellations of listing by judicial review (R v Stock Exchange ex p Else (1992).

Unlisted securities

Companies which are inadmissible to the Official Listed Market may apply for admission to the Alternative Investment Market (A.I.M.). Offers of unlisted securities are governed by FSA 1986 Part V (FSA 1986 s158).

A person may not be responsible for the issue of an advertisement offering securities to be admitted to an approved exchange (R.I.E.) without the approval of the exchange and the delivery to the Registrar (FSA 1986s 159) of a prospectus. Similarly, a prospectus must be registered if the person is responsible for the issue of an advertisement for securities which is a primary offer (i.e. one inviting the initial subscribing for or underwriting of securities) or a secondary offer (i.e. by a person who has acquired shares from a purchaser) though the Secretary of State can make an exemption in cases where the general public is unlikely to require the relevant information. Prospectuses must contain information prescribed by rules made by the Secretary of State and must contain all such information as investors and their professional advisors would reasonably expect to make an informed assessment of the present and anticipated rights and financial status of the securities (FSA 1986 ss163 and 164). Advertisements may not be issued for securities in private companies.

The main statutory rules are enhanced by the Public Offers of Securities Regulations 1995, which implement the E.C. Prospective Directive. They regulate first timer public offers of unlisted securities, subject to a number of exceptions (e.g. for denominations of less than ECU's 40,000). Free prospectuses must be published.

Subsequent dealings

A subsequent purchaser of securities on a market governed by the above rules should be protected by the securities having to comply with the rules governing the market. In addition, the ordinary law will also provide protection.

Criminal penalties and civil liability

The Financial Services Act, as amended, imposes a criminal liability for contravention of certain provisions. In addition it is an offence fraudulently or recklessly to induce someone to deposit money with any person (Banking Act 1987 s35). Under the Theft Act 1968 s19 a company officer causing or contributing to publication of a statement knowing it to be false or misleading, with intent to deceive members or creditors, may be imprisoned.

Civil liability

Whether on a first issue of or a subsequent dealing with shares, a person relying on a false statement may have a remedy against the company or the individual responsible. The following rules also apply:

- A person subscribing for or purchasing shares on the basis of misrepresentation may rescind the contract. The remedy is subject to the usual bars and to the courts discretion to award damages in lieu.
- Damages for breach of contract are unlikely to be available against the company, mainly because of the rules governing the maintenance of capital and equal rights of membership, but such damages might be claimed from a transferor of shares.
- A person intending to rely and actually relying on a false representation made knowingly or without belief in its truth or recklessly may sue for damages for deceit, but a purchaser of shares in the market cannot sue if the representation is made as an inducement only to original subscribers unless it is also meant to

mislead subsequent purchasers or is reactivated by a later statement.

- A defendant issuing a prospectus may be liable for damages for negligence to a subsequent purchaser of the companies shares on the unlisted securities market if the defendant intended subsequent purchasers to rely on the prospectus.

- At least before liquidation begins, a person is now no longer debarred from obtaining compensation from a company simply by virtue of his status as a holder for applicant, or subscriber for, shares. The Financial Services Act 1986 entitles a person to receive compensation for loss caused by false listing particulars and prospectus without having to relinquish his membership.

- A person acquiring securities on the basis of a false statement in listing particulars or a prospectus may claim compensation from persons responsible subject to defences of reasonable belief, ignorance or disclaimer.

- Damages for breach of statutory duty might be recoverable for omission of statutorily required details from prospectuses and courts have a discretion to award compensation in criminal proceedings.

The raising and maintenance of capital-statement of capital

Companies can raise capital to finance activities in a number of ways. The deferral of payments, through the acquisition of items on hire purchase or lease terms is one way. For the raising of substantial sums a company will need to obtain loans at preferential rates and will, more often than not, issue debentures, a form of promise to pay at a fixed rate of interest. Debentures can be attractive, depending on interest rates and tax advantages. Debentures will be discussed in greater depth a little later.

Companies will issue shares to raise capital. This is another very common method of financing. Shares are split into different classes of preference share providing different returns and levels of security to appeal to different types of investor. The rights of any preference shareholder are limited to the terms of issue of the class of share allotted. A dividend may be paid following from which there is no entitlement to share in any further income. Shares may be redeemable (at any point) in which case the shareholder cannot vote at meetings. The class of share will determine the rights, obligations and ultimate gains of the shareholder.

Share capital can be nominal, in other words the amount of money the company's memorandum entitles the company to raise. This can comprise issued share capital and un-issued share capital. Paid up capital represents the money actually received from shares sold and uncalled capital the amount owed.

Reserve capital is uncalled capital which the company has resolved only to call up on liquidation (Companies Act 2006). Shares may be issued at a premium (for more than their nominal value) if so the extra value must be transferred to a share premium account. Profits undistributed as income are kept in a reserve fund.

The liability of members of limited companies is limited to the nominal value of their shares. The nominal value of a public company's share capital must not be less than the authorised minimum, currently £50,000 (Companies Act 2006). One quarter of the value of all issued shares of a public company plus any premiums must be paid up. Shares must not be issued at a discount although debentures may.

A commission may be paid to underwriters. Shares may be allotted for money or moneys worth. If shares are allotted for moneys worth, the consideration for allotment must be valued by an expert, whose report must be made to the company and made available to the allotee. Capital cannot be returned to members by the company. In general a company cannot acquire its own shares, subject to some exceptions (CA 2006 s 658).

A company must not provide financial assistance to another to acquire its or its holding company's shares. There are unconditional exceptions to this principle in s 681 of the CA 2006:

a) a distribution of the company's assets by way of a dividend lawfully made, or a distribution in the course of a company's winding up;

b) an allotment of bonus shares;

c) a reduction of capital'

d) a redemption of shares;

e) anything done in pursuance of an order of the court sanctioning compromise or arrangement with members or creditors;

f) anything done under an arrangement made in pursuance of s 110 of the Insolvency Act 1986;

g) anything done under an arrangement made between a company and its creditors that is binding on the creditors by virtue of Part 1 of the Insolvency Act 1986.

There are further exceptions for public companies in s 682 of the CA 2006:

- Companies may reduce their capital by passing a special resolution to this effect and obtaining the consent of the court to the reduction (s 641 (1) of the CA 2006)

- If a public company suffers a serious loss of capital (net assets worth half or less of called up share capital) then a general meeting is required to be called to alert the shareholders within 28 days of discovering that the loss of capital has occurred. The meeting should take place within 56 days (s 656 of the CA 2006).

Dividends to shareholders

Under s 820 the rules of the CA 2006 (from 2008) apply to 'every description of a company's assets to its members, whether in cash or otherwise'. Section 830 (2) of the CA 2006 provides that distributions can only Section 831 of the CA 2006 applies to public companies. It requires the public company to maintain the capital side of its account in addition to having available profits. Therefore, if the company's net assets are worth less than the subscribed share capital plus undistributable reserves at the end of the trading period, that shortfall must first be made good out of distributable profits before a dividend can be made. If a dividend is wrongly paid, a member may be liable to repay it under s 847 of the CA 2006.

Directors who are responsible for unlawful distributions can be held liable for breach of duty. If the directors have relied on auditors in recommending a dividend, then the auditors may be liable.

Changes made by the The Small Business, Enterprise and Employment Act 2015

From June 2016, the Statement of Capital will be simplified. The changes remove the requirement to show the amount paid up and unpaid on each share. Instead, director(s) now need to show the aggregate amount unpaid on the total number of shares. This figure is more useful for shareholders and creditors as it shows money which is still due to the company.

Currently, a statement of capital needs to be provided every year on the annual return. Instead, it can now simply be shown on the confirmation statement that there have been no changes for that year. Director(s) will only need to provide a full statement of capital where changes have been made during the year. This will avoid having to provide duplicate information to the registrar.

Becoming a shareholder

A person can become a shareholder by subscribing to a company, as per its memorandum or having shares transferred to him by an existing shareholder. Companies must keep a register of the class and extent of the company's shareholdings. A share is an item of property and usually freely transferable. It gives the holder an interest in the company measured by a sum of money and entitling him to the rights contained in the articles of association. The value of the shares is generally their market price although a large number whose votes confer more may have a greater value.

Shareholders would usually have equal rights but companies can issue various classes of shares depending on the articles of association. The nominal value of a share specifies the maximum liability of a member of a company. A share in a public company must be paid up by at least 25 percent but the company can make calls on the holder up to its unpaid value.

The articles may give the company a lien over the share for calls on the holder up to the unpaid value. They often empower it to forfeit the share for unpaid calls. A lien is an equitable charge on the share. It becomes effective on a specified event. Thus a different equitable interest of which the company has interest overrides a lien for debts due from the member (which it could set off against dividends) if the member only becomes indebted after the interest arose.

Under the Companies Act 2006, a company must, within two months of the allotment of shares or debentures or within two months of the lodging of a transfer of such securities, complete certificates, unless it is otherwise provided in their original issue, or it is not entitled to a certificate by virtue of the Stock Transfer Act 1982 (governing transfer of securities through a computerised system), or the allotment is to or the lodging of transfer is with a Stock Exchange nominee, or it is excused under the Uncertificated Securities Regulations 1995.

Transfer and transmission of securities
Formal documentation is usually necessary for the transfer of shares. However, the Secretary of State has been authorised to provide by regulation for title to securities to be evidenced and transferred without a written instrument. Otherwise shares are freely transferable. Articles of association may restrict transfer in which case a refusal to register must be made within two months of its being lodged and must not be made in bad faith. The seller

should transfer his share certificate to the buyer so that the company will readily consent to registering him as a member. If the seller only transfers part of his holding, he should deposit his share certificate with the stock exchange (if PLC) or the company, which will issue a certificate of transfer. Fully paid registered securities may be transferred by a stock transfer form approved under the Stock Transfer Act 1963. For a transfer to be registered by the company, unless the transfer is exempted by the Stock Transfer Act 1982, an instrument of transfer must be delivered to the company by either the transferor or the transferee.

Insider dealing

In recent years in particular, there has been controversy over the use of confidential information affecting the values of securities which is taken into account by the person in possession of it in deciding whether to buy or sell shares so as to make a profit. Insider trading, the use of knowledge by people on the inside of companies is seen as commercially immoral. However, it is extremely difficult to prevent. The only real deterrent is to impose criminal sanctions and to increase the powers of the various regulatory bodies.

The Stock Exchange requires listed companies to adopt its Model Code for Securities Transactions for Directors and to secure compliance with it. The Code warns directors to avoid insider dealing and requires them to refrain from dealing within two months before announcement of the company's results and to notify the company of such dealings.

The common law position in relation to insider dealing is based on Percival v Wright (1902). Shareholders offered to sell shares to directors who knew their true value was greater because of an impending takeover bid, which information their confidential obligations to the company forbade them to disclose. For that reason it was decided that the shareholders could not rescind the contract. The directors had no general duty to the shareholders to disclose price sensitive information to them. The Companies Act 2006 imposes a statuary prohibition by making it a criminal offence for a director to purchase an option to buy or sell quoted shares or debentures to a company in his group. This liability is extended to his wife and children unless they had no reason to believe he was a director.

The Companies Act also enacts requirements for disclosure and publicity. A director must disclose to the company details concerning the acquisition or disposal of any beneficial interest to himself, his wife or children in the group. If the shares are quoted the company must pass the information on to the stock exchange which may publish it. Any shareholders knowingly acquiring or disposing of a notifiable interest in voting shares (5 percent) in a public company must notify the company, which must keep a register of such interests.

There is also some administrative control.. Under the CA 2006, the Secretary of State can appoint inspectors to investigate suspected breaches of the various areas of the Companies Act.

The Financial Services Act 1986, as amended

There are certain provisions of the Financial Services Act that may apply to insider dealing. A private investor or other person suffering a loss from breach of a relevant rule may sue for damages for breach of statutory duty under the Financial Services Act ss61-62A.

The Criminal Justice Act 1993 Part V

If an individual knowingly has information which is insider information then he commits an offence if:

- Where the acquisition or disposal occurs on a regulated market, or where he acts or relies on a professional intermediary, he deals price affected securities.
- He encourages another person to deal in such securities knowing or having reasonable cause to believe that the

acquisition or disposal occurs on a regulated market, or that the person dealing acts as or relies on a professional intermediary.

- He discloses the information to another person other than in the proper performance of his employment, office or profession.

The offence is punishable by a fine and/or up to seven years imprisonment. The Act has other provisions which provide for further sanctions and defences.

Borrowing money

In addition to issuing shares a company can raise finance by borrowing money. This is usually done in the longer term by issuing debentures. A Company may create a debenture fund and issue certificates for particular parts of the fund. The rights of debenture holders are fixed by the contract governing the loan. This is incapable of being altered even if, along the way, the articles are altered. Any attempted alterations represent a breach of contract.

Charges

Any form of security interest (fixed or floating) other than an interest arising by operation of law, is for the purposes of the Companies Act 2006 (Registration of charges) known as a charge.

Fixed and floating charges

A company can create a fixed charge over part of its property for the amount of the loan. Where a fixed charge is inappropriate, i.e. over fluctuating assets a floating charge over the whole or part of the company's assets can be made. The value of the charge as security depends on the assets in the company's possession at the time.

A charge must be registered within 21 days of its creation or the acquisition of property subject to it. The company and any officer at fault may be fined for non-registration. The court has discretion to extend a registration period. The Companies Act 2006 lists the registrable charges, including those on land, goods, intangible moveable property, i.e. intellectual property, for securing issues of debentures and floating charges. Not every charge is registrable, this very much depends on the nature of the charge.

Effects of non-registration

Where a registrable charge created by the company is not registered, the security is void against an administrator or liquidator of the company and any person who for value acquires an interest in or right over property subject to the charge where the beginning of insolvency proceedings, or acquisition occurs after the charge's creation. Where the registered particulars are not complete or accurate the charge is void, unless a court orders otherwise.

A registered charge, in general, gives the chargee a prior right, according to its terms, over a subsequent charge and any previous unregistered charges. But a subsequent floating charge can be created over a particular part of the assets covered by a previous floating charge over the wider category. A later fixed charge will gain priority over a previous floating charge covering the assets in question. In either case this is because floating charges are created with knowledge of the possibility of subsequent dealings with assets.

Unregistered chargees may prove in a company's liquidation as unsecured creditors and rank in priority as such. Fixed chargees can simply enforce their security according to the terms of the charge. The rights of floating chargees are, however, postponed to those entitled to preferential payments on a winding up (s196).

A floating charge created within 12 months of the onset of insolvency (24 months if in favour of a person connected with the company) or between the presentation of a petition for and the consequent making of an administration order is, unless the charge is not connected with the company and the company was solvent immediately after its creation, void except to the amount of any consideration provided simultaneously with or subsequent to its creation, plus interest.

****

Ch. 5

Business Law-Intellectual Property-Patents

Historical background to patents and patent law

Patents were originally granted by the Crown exercising its Royal Prerogative. Letters patents were a royal proclamation that the bearer had the Crown's authority to do whatever had been authorised within the letters. The earliest record of a granted patent dates from 1331, to a Flemish weaver who wanted to practice his trade in England. Most of the patents granted at the time were to encourage trade rather than new inventions. In many cases, the grant of a patent was a way of controlling trade and towards the end of Elizabeth 1's reign, there were many abuses of the system.

The Statute of Monopolies 1623 was passed to control or limit these abuses. Monopolies per se were excluded unless they came within the exception in s.6. Under s.6 a 14-year monopoly could be granted for 'any manner of new manufacture'. The Patents Act 1835 was passed to deal with disclaimers and prolongations of claim, but the first comprehensive statute on the subject was the Patent Law Amendment Act 1852 which set up the Patent Office and Registrar of Patents. The Act also introduced the important requirement that a 'specification' be filed with an application describing the nature of the invention.

In 1883, the Patents, Designs and Trade Marks Act was passed to enable the United Kingdom to satisfy its obligations of reciprocity under the Paris Convention for the protection of Industrial Property. This Act required a full specification including detailed claims to be completed by the applicant and examined by the Patent Office before a patent would be granted. The case of

Nobel's Explosive Company Limited v Anderson (1894) established that it was no longer possible to claim that the patent extended to matter contained within the specification where such matter was not in the claim. This highlighted the use of claims to mark the legal boundaries of the claim.

At this point in time, the United Kingdom patenting system was purely a deposit system, where applications were checked simply to make sure they had been completed correctly. The need to prove that an invention was really new did not come until the passing of the Patents Act 1907 which introduced the practice of checking patents for novelty, with searches being extended to cover patents granted over the last 50 years. The grounds for declaring a patent invalid were codified in the 1907 Act. In the 1919 Patents Act it was stated that invalid claims within an application would not invalidate the whole application.

The entire patents system was overhauled in 1949 by the Patents Act 1949, and the modern law on patents is set down in the Patents Act 1977, as amended by:

- the Copyright Design and Patents Act 1988
- the Patents and Trade Marks (World Trade Organisation) Regulations 1999
- the Patents Regulations 2000
- the Enterprise Act 2002
- the Regulatory Reform (Patents Order) 2004
- the Patents Act 2004
- the Medicines (Marketing Authorisations etc.) Amendment Regulations 2005
- the Intellectual Property (Enforcement, etc.) Regulations 2006
- the Patents (Compulsory Licensing and Supplementary Protection Certificates) Regulations 2007
- the Legal Services Act 2007
- the Crime and Courts Act 2013

- the Enterprise and Regulatory Reform Act 2013(Competition) (Consequential, Transitional and Saving Provisions) Order 2014
- the Copyright (Public Administration) Regulations 2014
- the Intellectual Property Act 2014
- the Legislative Reform (Patents) Order 2014, and the Patents (Supplementary Protection Certificates) Regulations 2014. The Intellectual Property Act 2014 became law from October 2014 and was fully implemented by the end of 2015. Key changes to patent law include

- marking patented products with a web address
- expansion of the patent opinions service
- patents worksharing

Finally, the Intellectual Property (Unjustified Threats) Act 2017, which came into effect on 1st October 2017.

In this book, we are covering the essence of patents and the law covered by the 1977 Act as amended plus making reference to the Intellectual Property (Unjustified Threats) Act 2017.

The meaning of 'patent'
As we saw earlier, a patent is a monopoly right. The product or process, which is being patented, must first satisfy the criteria of the Patents Act 1977, which are:

1. There must be an invention, which must be capable of being patented but not an 'as such' invention. Certain inventions are non-patentable. This arises out of the Patents Act 1977 s1 (2) and (3)) The statute does not provide a clear definition of invention but the Patents Act sets out a list of things that are considered to be inventions 'as such': general abstract entities, aesthetic

and non-technical things are considered to be excluded. Discoveries, scientific theories and other things such as mathematical methods are not considered to be inventions 'as such'.

2.   One of the most problematic areas to arise out of this definition of things that are not regarded as being true inventions is that of computer programs. Despite not being considered inventions under the PA 1977 it is the case that patents for software related inventions are indeed granted. Software patents are granted when a substantial technical contribution is made, as this is not considered to be a computer program as such. One of several approaches is taken when deciding whether there has been a technical contribution:

i)   The question should be asked whether technical means are used to produce a result or solve a problem

ii)   Does the invention produce a technical result

- Novelty must be present in the product or process which distinguishes it from other products and processes (PA 1977 s.2)
- An inventive step must be present, i.e. the product or process must be seen as containing an clear element of invention (PA 1977 s. 3)
- The invention must be capable of industrial application, i.e. must be of a purpose which can be applied to some form of industry (PA 1977 s.4)

Other areas of enterprise are not patentable 'as such'. Mental acts, schemes, rules playing a game or business methods.

Mental acts. In Raytheon (1993) an apparatus and process was claimed for the identification of ships. This involved the digital composition of the silhouette of the unknown ship with silhouettes of known ships, held in a computer memory. The claim was held to be excluded as it was merely an automation of a method normally carried out by individuals, i.e. a mental act as such. Carrying out the method with a computer did not create a technical effect.

Schemes, rules or methods for playing a game. Innovations in this area do not really amount to a technical contribution.

Business methods. The courts in the UK have always taken a strict approach to the patentability of business methods. Inventions must make a technical contribution but that contribution must not be in an excluded thing (such as a business method) and it is also seen that advances in business methods are not technical. More recent European patent office developments indicate that a more relaxed approach may be adopted. Whilst process claims to business methods are not inventions, 'as such' product claims may be patentable.

The presentation of information

The Patents Act 1977 s.1 (2)(d) provides that means of presenting information are not inventions 'as such'.

Non-Patentable Inventions

In some cases, rare though they may be, the commercial exploitation of an invention may be contrary to public policy or morality. Such an invention is unpatentable. The European Patent Office in Harvard/Onco-mouse (1991) when considering the patentability of a mouse or other non-human mammal genetically engineered so as to be predisposed to develop cancer, suggested that this should be addressed as a balancing exercise. Here the suffering of the mouse and the possible environmental risks were felt to be outweighed by the utility of the invention to humans, hence the Onco-mouse was not immoral.

As public policy and morality objections proved particularly problematic in the field of biotechnology, Directive 09/44/EC on the legal protection of Biological Invention provides further guidance on what is not patentable:

1) The formation and development of the human body and mere discoveries of elements of the human body (this includes gene sequences) are not patentable. However, where a technical process is used to isolate or produce elements (including genes) from the human body, this may be patentable.

2) Processes for modifying human germ line genetic identity (i.e. genetic changes that can be passed to the next generation.

3) Human cloning processes.

4) Genetic engineering of animals which is likely to cause the animal to suffer without a substantial medical benefit, either to man or to animals.

5) Plant or animal varieties or biological processes for the production of such varieties are not patentable, but inventions concerning plants or animals may be patented where the invention is not confined to a particular variety.

The concept of novelty

As discussed earlier, an invention must be novel (Patents Act 1977 s.1(1)(a) In UK patent law the terms 'novelty' and 'anticipation' are used interchangeably.

An invention must be new in the sense that it must not previously have been made available to the public. The Patents Act 1977 s.2 (1) provides that an invention is novel where it does not form part of the state of the art. Anticipation is judged by asking 'is the invention part of the state of the art'? Novelty is assessed objectively. In order for an invention to be anticipated, the prior art must either contain an enabling disclosure (in the case of a product patent) or, for process patents, it must give clear and unmistakable directions to do what the applicant has invented.

A key case here is Lux Traffic Controls Ltd v Pike Signals Ltd (1993) concerning what use amounts to disclosure to the public.. It was claimed that a temporary traffic signal was not 'new' because it had bee made available to the public in a paper, by oral disclosure, and by the use of a prototype which had been tested in public in Somerset.

The main principle to emerge from the case was that a prior publication must contain clear and unmistaken directions to do what the patentee claims to have invented: a signpost will not suffice. Where prior use is concerned there is no need for a skilled person to actually examine the invention as long as they were free in law and equity to do so and if a skilled person had seen it they would have been able to understand what the inventive concept was.

State of the art

The Patents Act 1977 s.2 (2) defines the state of the art as comprising all matter made available to the public before the priority date of the invention, this being the date of the first patent application. It therefore comprises all knowledge, global, on the subject matter of the invention. This knowledge can be made available in any way, either written, orally, or by any other means before the priority date.

The state of the art includes matter included in earlier patent applications, including those patent applications that are not yet published. Everything in the state of the art is known as prior art. Novelty destroying prior art could include information that is part of common general knowledge as well as specific pieces of prior art.

In some circumstances, a known invention may still be patented where a new use for that invention can be found, for example first medical use (Patents Act 1977) which provides that the first medical use of a known compound is novel, providing that the medical application of the compound does not itself form part of the state of the art (s.2 (6)). Also second medical use. In Europe a policy has developed of allowing second and subsequent uses of known compounds. Such claims are novel where the second or subsequent medical use does nor form part of the state of the art and provided the patent application takes a very narrow form known as a Swiss Form Claim i.e. the use of medicament X for treatment of disease Y. The UK courts have sanctioned the use of Swiss Form Claims, but second and subsequent medical uses will only be novel in the UK, where there is a new therapeutic application, discovering information about a medical use is sufficient.

The Inventive step

An invention that is patentable must involve an inventive step. An inventive step is present where an invention would not be obvious to a person skilled in the art. In patent law, the term's 'inventive step' and 'non-obviousness' are used interchangeably.

Inventive steps are assessed from the perspective of the person skilled in the art (PA 1977 s.3), the skilled man. This hypothetical person has certain attributes, he is the average person in the relevant art, possessing the relevant skills, knowledge and qualifications. The statutory test for inventive step is embodied in what is know as the 'windsurfer' test. This test follows the approach set out in Windsurfer v Tabur Marine (1983) as modified by PLG Research Ltd v Ardon International Ltd (1995). According to the Windsurfer test, to test obviousness the following should be asked:

1) What is the inventive step involved in the patent?
2) At the priority date, what was the state of the art relevant to that test?
3) How does the step differ from the state of the art?

4) Without hindsight, would the taking of the step be obvious to the person skilled in the art?

When attempting to obtain a patent, it is important to note that patents are territorial rights, not universal and therefore it is necessary to apply for patents in each jurisdiction for which protection is desired. For example, a UK patent may be obtained from the Intellectual Property Office. Although there is currently no 'European Patent' as such, a so called 'bundle' of patents, national patents, from states that are party to the European Patents Convention 1973 (EPC) may be obtained by a single patent application to the European Patent Office.

The employee inventor – ownership of patents

When a patent is applied for, the basic rules are that a patent must be granted to the following:

1) The inventor or joint inventors i.e. the actual devisor of the invention. (Patent Act 1977 s.7(2) (a)
2) The inventor(s) successors in title
3) The employer of an employee inventor.

Ownership of employee inventions

Inventors have the right to be mentioned as such but the Patent Act 1977 provides that where the inventors are employees their employer will own the invention if:

a) The invention was made in the course of the employee's normal duties or in the course of specially assigned duties, provided that he or she might reasonably be expected to carry out those duties.
b) Where the employee has a special obligation to further the interests of his employer's undertaking. This is related to the duty of fidelity that the employer owes to his or her employer.

Where the invention belongs to the employer, statutory compensation of the employer inventor may be available (PA 1977 s.40) provided that the patent is of outstanding benefit to the employer, the invention is subject of a patent grant and that it is just that compensation should be awarded.

There is a very high ceiling for statutory compensation and there has never actually been a reported case where statutory compensation under the 1977 act has been awarded. This is because such disputes tend to be settled out of court.

Patent applications may fail or those that are granted may be withdrawn on the basis of what is known as 'sufficiency'. A patent application consists of a number of components, and the patent specification is a vital part in which the invention is described and defined, it is the source of all the information about the patent that reaches the public domain. The specification must disclose the invention in such a way that the invention could be performed by the person skilled in the art. In other words, the application must contain an enabling disclosure.

The patent claim itself determines the scope of the monopoly granted to a patent proprietor. Claims must be clear and concise, be supported by the description and relate to a single inventive concept (PA 1977 s.14 (5).

Infringement of a patent

Certain activities carried out in the United Kingdom without permission of the patent holder constitute infringement (Section 60(1) and (2) of the Patents Act 1977:

1) Primary infringement. This falls into three categories:
   i) where a product patent is at issue, making, disposing of, using, importing or keeping the patented product (or disposal or otherwise)
   ii) where a process patent is at issue, use of the process with actual or constructive knowledge

       that non-consensual use constitutes
       infringement

  iii)   The use, offer to dispose of, importation or keeping for disposal or otherwise of a product directly obtained from a patented process.

2) Contributory infringement. The supply or offer to supply any of the means that relate to an essential element of the invention, for putting the invention into effect may constitute infringement. This will only be the case where there is actual or constructive knowledge that those means are suitable (and are intended) for putting the invention into effect in the UK.

Exceptions to infringement

There are a number of exceptions to patent infringement set out in the Patent Act 1977 s.60 (5)(a)-(i) the main ones being:

- Private and non-commercial use
- Experimental use

The courts have considered whether repairs to patented products constitutes infringement. The position is quite clear, genuine repair of a patented product that has been sold for use does not constitute infringement. Anyone who wishes to attack a patent by claiming for revocation can do so on the grounds that the patent is not a patentable invention 'as such' or the invention is contrary to public policy or morality, the person granted the patent is not the person entitled to the patent, the patent specification does not amount to an enabling disclosure or there has been an impermissible amendment to the patent (PA 1977 s.72).

The Intellectual Property (Unjustified Threats) Act 2017

The Intellectual Property (Unjustified Threats) Act 2017 (the "Act") received Royal Assent on 27 April 2017 and applies from 1 October 2017, making a number of amendments to the Patents Act 1977.

The Act

The Act has three key aims: (i) to protect businesses and individuals against the misuse of threats to intimidate or gain an unfair commercial advantage where there has been no infringement; (ii) to make it easier for those involved in an IP infringement dispute to negotiate a settlement, and avoid litigation; and (iii) bring consistency across the law of unjustified threats as it applied to patents, trademarks and designs.

There are a number of changes to the law surrounding unjustified threats as a result of the Act, in particular it:

- creates a new statutory test for what is a "threat of infringement proceedings";
- allows for threats to be made by "mass communication" methods;
- creates a new safe-harbour for "permitted communications";
- updates the permissible defences, to include situations in which no primary actor in an infringement can be found, despite "reasonable steps" being taken;
- creates an exception for professional advisers, under certain circumstances; and
- creates provisions for unjustified threats in relation to a unitary patent.

Threat Test

The Act modifies the "threat test", introducing an objective, two-step test to determine whether a communication amounts to a "threat of infringement proceedings". This requires that a reasonable person in the position of a recipient of the threat would understand from the communication that:

- a patent exists; and
- a person intends to enforce the patent against another person (in the UK or elsewhere) for an actual or potential infringement in the UK.

Threats need no longer be understood to relate only to bringing infringement proceedings in the UK. As a result, the provisions will apply to the unitary patent and the Act also inserts a new Schedule into the Patents Act 1977 in respect of unitary patents, for when the UPC Agreement comes into force. Furthermore, the new threat test ensures that threats to bring proceedings before the UPC in respect of patents falling within its jurisdiction will, where appropriate, fall within the scope of the threat provisions.

Who may bring an action?

It remains the law that: (i) any person "aggrieved" by a threat may bring an action; and (ii) such a threat is not actionable if it is made in respect of making or importing a product for disposal, or for using a process. In these cases, it is also not actionable to threaten proceedings for any other alleged infringement in respect of the product or process.

The Act also provides protection against threats made through mass communication, such as press releases. Such threats do not have to be directed at a particular individual.

Safe-Harbour

The Act provides a "safe harbour" to allow a patent holder to communicate with someone who might otherwise be entitled to bring an unjustified threats action if threatened. The "permitted communication" must be done for a "permitted purpose". A communication containing a threat of infringement proceedings is a "permitted communication" if:

- the communication is made solely for a "permitted purpose";
- all the information provided is necessary for that purpose; and
- the person making the communication reasonably believes it is true.

Permitted purposes include:

- notifying the recipient that the patent right exists;
- attempting to discover whether and by whom the patent is infringed (by making or importing a product, or using a process); and
- giving notice that a person has a right under a patent where that person's awareness of the patent is relevant to the action that may be taken.

The Act also grants the court the power to treat any other purpose as a "permitted purposes" if it is in the "interests of justice". The aim of this is to provide certainty over what will be considered a permitted purpose, whilst allowing the court the flexibility to take the surrounding circumstances of a case into account. The Act also lists purposes which cannot be considered "permitted purposes".

Defences and Exemptions

The old defence for making threats to secondary actors is retained, but reformed to the extent that the threatener must first use reasonable steps to discover the primary actor who is making or importing the product, or using the process. The person making the threat must also inform the person threatened either before or at the time of making the threat of the reasonable steps used.

It is also a defence to show that the act for which the threat was made is an actual or potential infringement.

Lawyers and registered patent attorneys are not liable for making threats where they have acted in their professional capacity on instructions from their client and have made that client known.

For details of changes to intellectual property law and patents after BREXIT go to:

https://www.gov.uk/government/news/intellectual-property-after-1-january-2021

5.2

Trade Marks

Definition of a trademark and historical background

A trademark is a symbol or a sign placed on, or used in relation to, one trader's goods or services to distinguish them from similar goods or services supplied by other traders. Section 1 of the Trade Marks Act 1994, as amended, which is the main legislation covering trade marks, defines a trade mark as any sign capable of being represented graphically which distinguishes the goods or services of one business from those of another.

The enactment of the 1994 Act radically changed the law dealing with registered trademarks. The legislation harmonises the trade mark law of the United Kingdom with that of the rest of the European Community and implements the first council directive (89/104/EEC) to approximate the laws of the member states relating to trademarks. The Government also took the opportunity with the 1994 Act to bring the law up to date, as the previous Act, the 1938 Act was inadequate in its scope and coverage.

From 14 January 2019 the long-awaited Trade Mark Directive (2015/2436) took effect in the UK, reflecting the UK's continued effort to enhance harmonisation of trade mark law across the EU. This is described below and also in the chapter on trademark applications.

Historical background

Traders have, from the earliest times, distinguished their goods by marking them. By the 19th century it had become very clear that marks applied to goods that had become distinctive had an intrinsic value and needed some form of legal protection lacking at the time.

Such protection was available through the use of Royal Charters and court action, which involved injunctions or action for infringement, although clearly this was not adequate or far reaching enough.

The Trademark Registration Act 1875 was passed to overcome the difficulties encountered in court actions. The Act established a statutory Register of Trademarks that is still in use today. The Register provides the trademark owner with proof of title to, and exclusive rights of use of, the trademark for the goods in respect of which it is registered. The Act of 1875 also laid down the essentials of a trademark. A number of Acts followed, the Patents, Designs and Trademarks Act 1883, the Trademarks Act 1905 and the Trademarks Act 1919. These Acts culminated in the 1938 Trademarks Act which in turn was replaced by the 1994 Trademarks Act.

International Provisions
There are a number of international conventions and arrangements that give some international recognition to national trademarks. These are the Paris Convention, The Madrid Arrangement and the Protocol to the Madrid arrangement (Madrid Protocol). There is also a Community Trademarks System that creates a trademark that gives rights throughout the European Community and which will be referred to below.

Paris Convention
The Paris Convention came into being in 1883. Its overall purpose was to create recognition between various countries of each other's national intellectual property rights, through the concept of priority.

Priority recognises the first filing date for a particular intellectual property right in any convention country as the filing date for all other convention countries in respect of the same property right. The period of priority differs from intellectual property right to intellectual property right but for trademarks the period is six months. This has given a level of international protection for trade marks because the first to file a trade mark application is, in most countries, the person with better claim to a trade mark.

In England, this is not the case because rights in passing off (see later) can be built up through sufficient use of a trademark, without registration, and these rights can act as an obstacle to any subsequent application to register the trademark by a third party.

Another provision of the Paris Convention relevant to trade marks is Article 6, which gives international protection to 'well known' trademarks. A person can own a well-known trademark in registered or unregistered form even in countries where the action of passing off does not exist. Ownership of a well known mark will prevent a third party from applying to register the same or similar mark in any other convention country that has implemented Article 6 and allows cancellation of an existing registration for such an identical or similar mark during the first five years after registration on the application of the owner of the well known mark.

The Madrid Agreement

The Madrid Agreement was implemented in 1891 to simplify the procedure for filing trademark registration in many countries. The Madrid Agreement aimed to replace the multiple filing of trademark registrations in (10) individual countries.

The Madrid Agreement allows anyone established or domiciled in an Agreement country, with a trademark registration in his or her country, to file one international application that will cover all Madrid Agreement countries. The central application is filed with the offices of the World Intellectual Property Rights Organisation (WIPO) in Geneva. This is then administered by that office. England did not sign the Madrid Agreement so this is not available to English trademark owners.

The Madrid Protocol

As a number of key countries did not sign the Madrid Agreement, discussions began in the mid-1980's on how to make the Madrid system more palatable. The result was the Madrid Protocol established in 1989. At the current time there are 42 signatories to the protocol including the UK. Up to date information concerning the countries and the protocol see www. Itma.org.uk

The protocol is based on essentially the same structure as the Madrid Agreement, with a few differences designed to allow more flexibility.

Although classed as an international registration system, the CTM operates differently from either the Madrid Agreement or Madrid Protocol. It is more like the national system (see below) in that it is a means of filing an application for one trade mark at one trade mark registry to obtain one registration under one set of laws and procedures. The only difference is that the area covered by the registration is a collection of countries within the European Union.

The application can be filed in The CTM Office in Alicante Spain or at the National Trademark office in any member country, which passes the application to the CTO Office.

Trademarks and registration of trademarks

As discussed, the function of a trademark is to distinguish between one trader's goods and another trader's goods. The function of an ordinary trade mark is to act as an indicator of trade origin, which aids both consumers of branded goods and the trade mark proprietor, as follows:

1) The trademark acts as an indicator of quality and reliability, protecting consumers from confusion or deception in the market place.

2) The trademark can be enforced to protect the mark's proprietor against certain acts of unfair competition.

Collective marks and certification marks

Although they are rare, such trademarks perform different functions compared to ordinary trademarks. Certification marks (Trademarks Act 1994 s.50) are intended to indicate that goods or services comply with a certain objective standard as to quality, origin, material, the mode of manufacture of goods or the performance of services or other characteristics. Any third party whose goods or services meet the required standards may apply to be an authorised user of a certification mark and the proprietor cannot refuse this request.

Collective marks serve to indicate members of an association. A third party who is not a member of that association does not have the right to use the mark. Collective marks can act as certification marks and vice versa.

Trademark law

As seen, in the UK, trademarks are governed by the 1994 Trademarks Act, as amended by the below:

The Trade Marks (EC Measures Relating to Counterfeit Goods) Regulations 1995 (SI 1995/1444) *(1 July 1995);*
Section 13 of the Olympic Symbol etc (Protection) Act 1995 *(21 September 1995);*
Part IV of the Patents and Trade Marks (World Trade Organisation) Regulations 1999 (SI 1999/1899) *(29 July 1999);*
Section 6 of the Copyright, etc. and TradeMarks (Offences and Enforcement) Act 2002 *(20 November 2002);*
The TradeMarks (Proof of Use, etc.) Regulations 2004 (SI 2004/946) *(5 May 2004);* $ the Trade Marks (International Registrations Designating the European Community, etc.) Regulations 2004 (SI 2004/2332) *(1 October 2004);*

The Serious Organised Crime and Police Act 2005 (*19 April 2005*); and
The Intellectual Property (Enforcement, etc.) Regulations 2006 (SI 2006/1028) *(29 April 2006).*
The Legal Services Act 2007
The Trade Marks (Relative Grounds) Order 2007
The TradeMarks (Earlier Trade Marks) Regulations 2008 (SI 2008/1067) (10 May 2008)
The Trade Mark Directive (2015/2436) effective from 14th January 2019)

An application for a national trademark may be made to the Intellectual Property Office (see next chapter). Community Trademarks (CTM), a trade mark that is valid in the entire EU, may be obtained from the CTM Office, The Office for Harmonisation in the Internal market (Trademarks and Designs) (OHIM). Not all marks are capable of being registered as trademarks. Objections to the registration of a mark may be raised, either by the IPO during examination of the mark or by third parties during any opposition actions or proceedings. The grounds for refusing registration are divided into two categories:

a) Absolute grounds for refusal (TMA 1994 s.3 and 4) which are concerned with objections based on the mark itself.
b) Relative grounds for refusal (TMA 1994 s.5) these being concerned with a conflict and third party rights.

Classification of a trade mark
The Nice Agreement for the International Classification of Goods and Services provides that there are thirty-four classes of goods and eight classes of services. Any application for registration must stipulate which classes, or sub-classes, in which registration is sought. Multi-class applications are possible and it would, in theory, be possible to register a mark in respect of all forty two classes.

However, this is very unlikely as applicants must have a bona fide intent to use the marks for the prescribed goods and services (TMA 1994 ss.3 (6) and 32 (3)).

Limited registration for retail service marks is also now possible in class 35. This change follows OHIM's decision in Giacomelli Sports Spa (1999).

Definition of a trade mark

The 1994 Trademarks Act s.1(1) provides that a trade mark is a sign capable of being represented graphically, capable of distinguishing goods or services of one undertaking, from those of another undertaking. There are a number of elements in the definition:

a) *A 'sign'.* The concept of a sign in UK trademark law is very broad indeed. Although there is no clear definition, signs provided in the UK include works, designs and shapes and also more unconventional marks such as sounds and smells. A sign can be regarded as anything that conveys information (Phillips v Remington (1998) See below.

b) *Graphic representation.* Signs must be represented graphically, i.e. be represented in such a way that third parties may determine and understand what the sign is,. This requirement is normally satisfied by including an image of the mark in the trade mark application. However, it has been suggested that provision of an image is not absolutely necessary provided that third parties can clearly identify the mark from the description (Swizzels Matlow Ltds Application (1999). It may be difficult to graphically represent unconventional marks, but practice dictates for example that sound marks are represented by music notation and that for shape marks it is best to submit line drawings or photographs. Applications for colour marks will usually include a representation of the colour and so on.

c) *Capable of distinguishing.* Signs must be capable of distinguishing goods or services of one undertaking from another undertaking. Any sign that has the capacity to distinguish will satisfy this requirement.

Absolute grounds for refusal

The main legislation is Section 3(1)(a-d) Trade Marks Act 1994, Art 3 (1) (a-d) Directive on the Legal protection of Trade marks. A sign will not be registered if it falls within one or more of the absolute grounds for refusing registration.

Signs not satisfying the s.1 (1) requirements

Signs which do not meet the definition of 'trade mark' provided in the Trademarks act 1994 will not be registered. In addition, it is important for an applicant not to make a mistake as to the graphic representation as the opportunities to correct or amend are very limited (TMA 1994 s.39 prevents the correction of errors in a trade mark application that would substantially affect the identity of the trade mark). This is mitigated by the fact that it is IPO practice to examine marks for graphic representation before a filing date is allocated.

Scent marks continue to cause considerable difficulties for graphic representation. John Lewis Application (The scent of Cinnamon) (2001) indicates a description of a scent is unlikely to be precise enough.

Signs must also be capable of distinguishing the goods or services of one undertaking form those of other undertakings. As noted above, this is not a high standard and, in effect, it will only bar those signs that are incapable of functioning as trademarks (e.g. the Philips shaver shape in Philips Electronics v Remington Consumer Products (1999) a case discussed below, was held not to be distinctive in a trade mark sense and thus did not satisfy TMA 1994, s.3 (1)(a)).

Marks devoid of distinctive character or those consisting of exclusively descriptive or generic signs are prohibited unless it can be shown that before the application was made, a mark has acquired a distinctive character as a result of a use made of it. This proviso to the TMA 1994 ss.3 (1)(b)(c) and (d) means that there is no absolute prohibition as a matter of law on non-distinctive, descriptive and generic marks. As recognised in British Sugar v James Robertson (TREAT) 1996, such marks may be registered where they have become factually distinctive upon use despite the provisions stated in the TMA 1994 s.3 (1)(b)-(d). This proviso does not apply to TMA 1994 s.3(1)(a) or any other absolute ground for refusal.

Marks devoid of distinctive character

TMA 1994 s.3 (1)(b) prevents the registration of marks that are not, prima facie, distinctive. An example might include a surname common in the UK. In British Sugar v James Robertson (TREAT) 1996, it was said that a mark is devoid of distinctive character where the sign cannot distinguish the applicants goods or services without the public being first educated that it is a trademark. The mark at issue in this case, TREAT, for a syrup for pouring on ice cream and desserts, was therefore devoid of distinctive character. Such marks may, nevertheless, benefit from the TMA 1994 s.3 (1)(b) proviso. Therefore trademarks will only fail where they are not distinctive by nature and have not become distinctive by nurture.

Signs that are exclusively descriptive

For a sign to be open to objection under TMA 1994 s.3 (1)(c) the trademark must consist exclusively of a sign which may be used in trade to describe characteristics of the goods or services. The sub-categories of TMA 1994 s.3 (1)(c) are:

1) Kind. Terms indicating kind or type that should be free for all traders to use, e.g. PERSONAL for computers, are not normally registrable.

2) Quality. Laudatory words, e.g. PERFECTION, are not usually registrable.

3) Quantity. The Trade Marks Registry gives the example that 454 would not be registrable for butter, as butter is frequently sold for domestic consumption in 454g (1lb) packs. Where numerical marks are not descriptive or otherwise objectionable, they may be registered.

4) Intended purpose. Generally, words referring to the purpose of goods or services are not registrable.

5) Value. Signs pertaining to the value of goods or services are not normally registrable, e.g. BUY ONE GET TWO FREE.

6) Geographical origin. Geographical names are not usually registrable unless used in specific circumstances.

7) Time of production of goods or the rendering of services. Typically, marks such as SAME DAY DELIVERY for courier services or AUTUMN 2004 for haute couture would not be registrable.

8) Other characteristics of goods and services. For example, a representation of the good or service would not usually be registrable.

Marks falling into any of these categories may still be registrable if they have become distinctive upon use.

Signs that are exclusively generic
TMA 1994 s.3(1)(d) prohibits the registration of signs or indications that have become customary in the current language or in the bone fide and established practices of the trade. An example can be found in JERYL LYNN Trademark (1999) where an application for JERYL LYNN for vaccines was refused as the mark described a strain of vaccine and was not distinctive of the applicant.

Shapes that cannot be registered

Traditionally in the UK, shapes were not registerable. One case highlighting this was Coca-Cola's trademark application (1986).

However, the TMA 1994 makes it very clear that the shapes of goods and their packaging are now registrable (TMA 1994 s.1 (1)), but the TMA 1994 s.3 (2) excludes certain shapes from registration. This is an area of trademark law that has lacked clarity. ECJ guidance on the registrability of shape marks has clarified matters somewhat. The UK Court of Appeal stayed proceedings in Phillips Electronics v Remington Consumer products (1999) to allow a preliminary reference to the ECJ in a number of issues, including questions specific to shape marks and this decision has implications for the interpretation of the TMA 1994 s.3 (2). In this case, Philips had been producing a three-headed rotary shaver for a considerable time (the Philishave). When Remington produced a rotary shaver of a similar design Philips sued for infringement of a mark which was the face of the three headed shaver.

The TMA 1994 provides that the following shapes are not registrable:

1) Where the shape results from the nature of the goods themselves. Inherent shapes therefore cannot be registered. In the Philips case, The Court of Appeal considered that there would be no objection to Philips three headed shaver shape on this ground as electronic shavers can take other forms.

2) Where the shape of the goods is necessary to achieve a technical result (TMA 1994 s.3 (2)(b). Functional shapes are therefore not registrable. In Philips 1999 case it was considered that the shaver shape was necessary to achieve a technical result, but the ECJ was, nevertheless, asked to adjudicate in the matter, i.e. on the correct approach to functional shapes. They concurred in the matter. They also confirmed that the fact that there may be more than one shape that could achieve the same result is not relevant.

Consequently, it appears that only shapes with specifically non-functional aspects are registrable.

3) Where the shapes gives substantial value to the goods. In Philips (1999) the Court of Appeal suggested that a valuable shape in this context can be identified where the shape itself adds substantial value, e.g. the shape adds value via eye appeal or functional effectiveness. In contrast, shapes that are valuable because they are 'good trademarks' would not fall foul of the TMA 1994.

Marks likely to give offence or deceive

A mark will not be registered if it is contrary to public policy or accepted principles of morality (TMA 1994 s.3 (3)(a) or is of such a nature that it is likely to deceive the public. For example, as to the nature, quality or origin of the goods or services.   Relatively few marks are deemed to be contrary to public policy or morality. Morality should be considered in the context of current thinking and only where a substantial number of persons would be offended should registration be refused..

For example, in BOCM's application, (EUROLAMB) (1997) EUROLAMB was considered to be deceptive if used in relation to non-sheep meat (when used in relation to sheep meat it was descriptive). It is very clear that the test of deception is deceptive and actual evidence of deception must be provided.

Marks prohibited by UK or EC law

The registration of marks whose use would be illegal under UK or Community law is precluded by TMA 1994 s.3(1)(d).

Protected emblems

TMA 1994 s.4 provides details of marks that are considered to fall into the category of specially protected emblems, e.g. marks with Royal connotations, and the Olympic symbol cannot be registered.

Marks containing such emblems cannot be registered without consent.

Applications made in bad faith

The key statute here is Section 3(3)(a) and (b) and section 3(6) Trade Marks Act 1994, Art 3(1)(f) and (2)(d) Directive on the Legal Protection of Trade Marks:

(3) A trade mark shall not be registered if it is -

(a) contrary to public policy or accepted principles of morality, or
(b) of such a nature as to deceive the public
(6) A trade mark shall not be registered if or to the extent that the application is made in bad faith.

There is no requirement that a mark need be used prior to the application for registration, but the applicant must have a bona fide intention to use the mark and applications may be refused when they are made in bad faith. Therefore, so-called ghost applications should be caught by this section.

Relative grounds for refusal

Section 5(1) Trade Marks act 1994, Art 4(1)(a) Directive on the Legal Protection of Trade marks:
(1) A trade mark shall not be registered if it is identical with an earlier trade mark and the goods or services for which the trade mark is applied for are identical with the goods or services for which then earlier trade mark is protected.
The applicant must also overcome the relative grounds for refusing registration. These relate to conflict with earlier marks or earlier rights. The 'earlier mark' (TMA 1994 s.6) might be a trademark registered in the UK or under the Madrid Protocol. Alternatively it might be a CTM or a well-known mark (the latter are entitled to

protection as per article 6 of the Paris Convention for the Protection of Industrial Property 1883).

There is no provision for honest concurrent use in the TMA 1994. As it has been made clear that a trade mark application must be refused, irrespective of honest concurrent use, if the registered proprietor objects, this provision is of limited value to the applicant. If the proprietor of the registered mark objects, honest concurrent use provides no defence.

Conflict with an earlier mark for identical goods or services

The TMA 1994 s.5 (1) only provides the narrowest relative ground for refusing registration: a mark identical to an earlier trademark and used for identical goods and services will not be registered. The requirement of 'identical goods and services' is sufficiently broad in scope to include cases where the applicants mark is identical to only some of the goods and services for which the earlier mark is registered, but to 'constitute an 'identical mark' a very high level of identity between the marks is required. One such case highlighting this is Origins Natural Resources v Origins Clothing (1995).

The registration of similar marks for the same or similar services is only prohibited where confusion on the part of the public is likely to arise (TMA 1994 s.5 (2). Specifically what is prohibited is the registration of:

1) Identical marks for similar goods or services or
2) Similar marks for identical/similar goods or services where, because of the identity or similarity, there is a likelihood of confusion on the part of the public, which includes the likelihood of association with the earlier trade mark.

What constitutes 'confusing similarity' has been considered at length by the ECJ (Sabel v Puma 1998) and Canon v Metro Goldwyn Meyer (1999). Confusion has to be appreciated globally taking into account all factors relevant to the case. These factors include:

- The recognition of the earlier trade mark on the market
- The association that can be made between the registered mark and the sign
- The degree of similarity between the mark and the sign and the goods and the services, the degree of similarity must be considered in deciding whether the similarity is sufficient so as to lead to a likelihood of confusion

It has also been made clear that 'likelihood of association' is not an alternative to 'likelihood of confusion" but serves to define its scope. This means that if the public merely makes an association between two trademarks, this would not in itself be sufficient for concluding that there would be a likelihood of confusion. There is no likelihood of confusion where the public would not believe that goods or services came from the same undertaking.

Conflict with a mark of repute

A mark that is identical or similar to an earlier mark will be refused registration in respect of dissimilar goods or services where the earlier mark is a mark of repute and the use of the later mark would, without the cause, take unfair advantage of or be detrimental to the reputed mark's distinctiveness or reputation. (TMA 1994 s5 (3).

A mark of repute is a mark with a reputation in the UK (for CTM applications it must have a reputation in the EU). In deciding as to whether a trade mark has a reputation, the ECJ has provided some guidance (General Motors Corp v Yplon) (2000). Repute would be judged with reference to the general public or to a specific section of the public, and the mark must be known to a significant portion of that public.

Relevant indicators of the public's knowledge of the mark include the extent and duration of the trade marks use, its market share and the extent to which it has been promoted.

In order for registration to be refused under s.5 (3) use of the applicants mark will have to take unfair advantage of or be detrimental to the reputed marks distinctiveness or reputation. In OASIS STORES LTD's application (EVEREADY) (1998) it was said that merely being reminded of an opponents mark did not itself amount to taking unfair advantage. The fact that the applicant did not benefit to any significant extent from their opponent's reputation and the wide divergence between the parties goods was relevant, s.5 (3) could not be intended to prevent the registration of any mark identical or similar to a mark of repute.

Conflict with earlier rights

TMA 1994 s.5 (4) provides that where a mark conflicts with earlier rights, including passing off, design rights and copyright the mark will not be registered.

Surrender, revocation, invalidity, acquiescence and rectification

Surrender. It is possible to surrender a trademark with respect to some or all of the goods or services for which it is registered. Marks may be revoked (removed from the registry on three grounds: non-use because the mark has become generic; or because the mark has become deceptive. A mark will be invalid if it breaches any of the absolute grounds for registration.

Where the proprietor of an earlier trade mark or other right is aware of the use of a mark subsequently registered in the UK and has, for a continuous period of five years, taken no action regarding that use the proprietor is said to have acquiesced. Where this is the case, the proprietor of the earlier mark or right cannot rely on his right in applying for a declaration of invalidity or in opposing the use of the later mark, unless it is being used in bad faith.

Anyone with sufficient interest can apply to rectify an error or omission in the register. Such a rectification must not relate to matters that relate to the validity of the trademark.

Infringement

Section 10(1) Trade Marks Act 1994, Art 5 (1)(a) Directive on the Legal Protection of Trade Marks:

'A person infringes a registered trade mark if he uses in the course of trade a sign which is identical with the trade mark in relation to goods or services which are identical with those for which it is registered'.

The proprietor (and any exclusive licensee) has certain rights to a mark (TMA 1994 s.9 (1) which are infringed by certain forms of unauthorised use of the mark in the UK. These rights come into existence from the date of registration, which is the date of filing. All infringement acts require the mark to be used in the UK in the course of trade. What constitutes 'use' of a mark has been the subject matter of some debate and is discussed below.

Use of an identical sign for identical goods or services

Use, in the course of trade, of an identical sign, in respect of goods or services constitutes trademark infringement (TMA 1994 s.10 (1).

Use of an identical or similar sign on identical or similar goods or services

Use, in the course of trade, of an identical sign or similar goods or services (TMA 1994 s.10 (2) (a) or a similar sign on identical goods or services constitutes infringement where the public is likely to be confused as to the origin of goods or services or is likely to assume that there is an association with the registered mark.

Use of a mark similar to a mark of repute for dissimilar goods or services

Registered marks with a 'reputation' are infringed if an identical or similar mark is used for non-similar goods or services, where the use takes unfair advantage of or is detrimental to, the distinctive character or repute of the distinctive mark (TMA 1994 s.10 (3).

256

Contributory infringement

TMA 1994 s.10 (5) is known as the contributory infringement provision. This provision creates a form of secondary participation where a person who applies a trademark to certain materials has actual or constructive knowledge that the use of the mark is not authorised. This provision extends infringement down the supply chain, but printers, publishers, manufacturers or packaging etc. may avoid a s. 10 (5) liability in practice by inserting suitable contractual forms into their agreement with their clients.

Defences to infringement

a) Comparative advertising. Comparative advertising is allowed under certain circumstances as long as the use is not unfair or detrimental. One such case that highlights this is British Airways PLC v Ryanair Ltd (2001). British Airways had brought an action for infringement against Ryanair for the publication of two Ryanair advertisements comparing fares with BA. The courts found that, in assessing as to whether a mark has been used in accordance with honest practice, the court should view the advertisement as a whole. Although misleading adverts cannot be honest, on the facts, whilst the advertisement at issue may have caused offence it was not dishonest and the price comparisons were not significantly unfair.

b) The use of another registered mark. The use of one registered mark, within the boundaries of the registration, does not infringe another registered mark.

c) Use of own name or address. A person using their own name or address does not infringe a registered mark, providing that the use accord with open honest practice. However, see the note on the Trade Mark Directive introduced in 2019.

d) Use of certain indications. The use of certain indications (e.g. the intended purpose of the gods or services or their

257

geographical origin) will not constitute infringement where that use accords with appropriate honest practice.

e) The locality defence. Signs applicable to a certain locality whose use predates the registration of a mark may continue to be used in that locality.

f) Exhaustion. Trademark rights are exhausted once the proprietor has consented to the placing of goods bearing the mark on the market within the EEA. For example, once a brand owner consents to a consignment of their goods being marketed in France, trademark rights cannot be used to prevent these goods from being resold in the UK, unless there are legitimate reasons for this. Goods sold in this way are known as 'grey imports' or parallel imports.

Please note that the Trade Mark Directive (2015/2436) introduced from 14th January 2019, make the following changes to infringement defences:

a. Own-name defence: the use of a trade mark as (or part of) a company name may now be found to be an infringing act. This defence now only applies if you are using your own personal name.

b. Non-use defence: As part of your defence during proceedings, you can now ask the owners of the registered mark to show that their mark is valid i.e. that they have been using it. This is easier than commencing parallel revocation proceedings based upon a claim of non-use.

c. If you applied to registered/started to use a mark that was similar/identical to an earlier registered once that mark had expired and then the owner of the earlier mark renews/restores it, they may now claim you are infringing this registration. Under certain circumstances, you may have a defence against such a claim.

In relation to invalidation proceedings, new amendments mean that the claimant may have to demonstrate more substantial evidence that their earlier rights are valid.

You should note that the Trade Mark Directive (2015/2346) introduced in january 2019 has introduced the following changes in respect of Trade Mark disputes:

1. In the event that you think fake or counterfeit goods under your mark are passing through the UK enroute to countries outside the customs territory of the EU, you can request that the customs authorities detain them. In any such dispute, it will now be up to the person shipping the goods to prove that you have no right to stop them being marketed in the destination country. (it is no longer required that the trade mark owner prove that the goods coming from the outside of the EU were intended to be put on sale in the UK). The burden of proof has now shifted to the importer.
2. Further to the above, a more extensive range of (counterfeit) activities will be treated as infringement. This should make it more difficult for parties that contribute to counterfeiting to avoid prosecution.
3. As the registered trade mark owner, you can now take action against publishers who have incorrectly identified your trade mark as a generic term in a dictionary etc. You may now ask the publisher to make it clear that the mark is registered, and if they fail to do so you can apply to the court to order that the publisher correct the entry or amend the entry, destroy copies of the publication, or order other remedies, as appropriate.
4. If someone acting as your trade mark agent or representative has applied for or registered your trade mark without your permission there are now provisions in

place for you to rectify the ownership on the Register as well as to invalidate the registration.

5. Prior to 14 January 2019, it was not possible to bring infringement proceedings against another registered mark unless you had firstly invalidated it. Now, the courts will consider invalidation-related issues during the course of infringement proceedings. Importantly, the courts will take into consideration the length of time you knew that the other was being genuinely used before taking legal action.

In addition to the above, the Directive has also introduced the following changes, which are als relevant to the next chapter:

If you licence use of your trade mark, it is now possible for you (as the trade mark owner) to take legal action under UK trade mark law, (as opposed to contract law) against the licensee if they fail to observe correctly the provisions in the licence which deal with how long the agreement lasts, what goods/services the licence covers, geographic area the mark can be used and quality etc.

Where previously, you were able to divide your application, it is now possible to divide registrations in the event of a dispute.

From 14 January 2019, the UK IPO will send out renewal reminders about 6 months before the renewal fee is due to be paid and your registration expires. Reminders were previously sent out about 4 months before the due date.

If you fail to renew your trade mark registration and you wish to 'restore' it, the UK IPO will now assess whether the registration should be restored based on whether the failure to renew was 'unintentional' (previously the test had been whether it was 'just' to renew your mark). The IPO will no longer have to consider other marks when deciding whether to restore your mark.

For details of changes to Trade mark Law after BREXIT go to:
https://www.gov.uk/government/news/intellectual-property-after-1-january-2021

5.3

Copyright

Definition of copyright

Copyright is the right to prevent others copying or reproducing an individuals or other's work. *Copyright protects the expression of an idea and not the idea itself.* Only when an idea is committed to paper can it be protected. Others can be directly or indirectly stopped from copying the whole or a substantial part of a copyright work. However, others cannot be stopped from borrowing an idea or producing something very similar.

Copyright is a right that arises automatically upon the creation of a work that qualifies for copyright protection. This means that there is no registration certificate to prove ownership. To claim ownership the author will have to produce original and preferably dated evidence of the creation of the work and proof of authorship. The author will also need to show that he is a qualifying person and that the work was produced in a convention country.

To be a qualifying person (s.154 of the Copyright Designs and Patents Act 1988) the author must have been, at the material time, a British Citizen, subject or protected person, a British Dependant territories citizen, a British national (overseas) or a British Overseas Citizen or must have been resident or domiciled in a convention country at the material time, which is when the work was first published. If the author dies before publication the material time is before his death. A convention country is a country that is signatory to the Universal Copyright Convention or the Berne Copyright Convention, which includes most countries in the world.

The works that can qualify for protection are defined in S.1 of the 1988 Act. These are:

a) Original literary, dramatic, musical and artistic works
b) Sound recordings, films, broadcasts and cable programmes
c) Typographical arrangements of published editions

Historical background

Copyright has its origins in the 16th century. The courts recognised a need for some form of protection for books. In 1556, a system of registration of books was established to offer protection for authors. If an author registered a book with the Stationers Company it gave him/her a perpetual right to reproduce the book and prevent reproduction by anyone else. For almost 200 years this form of protection only applied to books. In 1734 this extended to engravings (Engravings Copyright Act) A number of Acts were passed over the next 150 years extending copyright protection to musical, dramatic and artistic works. In 1875, a Royal Commission was set up to look at the position and recommended a clear approach be adopted to copyright protection, codified into one single Act. This happened after Great Britain signed the Berne Copyright Convention in 1885.

The Berne Convention provided for international protection of copyright for the work of all nationals of all countries signing the convention. It also required each member country to extend minimum standards of protection to nationals of all other member countries.

The United Kingdom implemented the 1911 Copyright Act to put into place minimum standards and also draw together previous legislation. The next Act, prompted by changes in the Berne Convention led to the 1956 Copyright Act. This Act reflected changes, amongst other things, in the field of technology. In 1973, the Whitford Committee was appointed to review the state of copyright law. The Committee reported in 1977 suggesting numerous changes to the law, resulting in a Green paper in 1981, 'Reform of the law relating to Copyright, Designs and Performers Protection' and subsequently the White Paper 'Intellectual

Property and Innovation' which led to the 1988 Copyright Designs and Patents Act, which was a consolidating Act and which has been amended.

Since the Act came into force in August 1989, there have been a number of amending regulations dealing with implementation of EC Directives on rights to reproduce copyright software as is necessary for lawful use, protection of semiconductor chip topography rights and harmonisation of copyright duration. There are further legislative moves afoot to update copyright law to deal with the growth of new technology. See the end of this chapter for an overview of significant amendments which have been made to the Act by new regulations introduced in 2014. The below deals with the main body of the 1988 Act.

Copyright – subsistence of copyright
As shown above, copyright is a property right that subsists in certain works. It is a statutory right giving the copyright owner certain exclusive rights in relation to his or her work.

In the 1988 Copyright Designs and Patents Act, as amended, there are nine categories of copyright works:

'Authorial' 'Primary' or 'LDMA' works
1) Literary works
2) Dramatic works
3) Musical works
4) Artistic works
5) 'Entrepreneurial' 'Secondary' or 'Derivative' works
6) Sound recordings
7) Films
8) Broadcasts
9) Cable programmes
10) Typographical arrangements of published editions (the typography right)

Copyright comes into existence, or subsists automatically where a qualifying person creates a work that is original and tangible (or fixed).

Qualification

Copyright will not subsist in a work unless:

a) It has been created by a qualifying person

b) It was first published in a qualifying country

c) In the case of literary, dramatic and musical works, the work must be fixed, that is reduced to a material form in writing or otherwise.

Copyright works

The CDPA 1988 defines a literary work as being 'any work written, spoken or sung, other than a dramatic or musical work'. A novel or poem could equally fall into this category. Additionally, the concept of literary works extends to tables (e.g. a rail timetable) compilations such as directories and computer programmes. Databases are also regarded as literary works. In essence, any work that can be expressed in print, irrespective of quality, will be a literary work.

Dramatic works

The CDPA 1988 defines 'dramatic works' as including works of dance or mime. In the case Norowzian v Arks (1999) it was stated that these terms should be given their natural and ordinary meaning, the implication being that dramatic works are works of *action*. The courts also recognised in this case that films may be produced as dramatic works, either as dramatic works in themselves and/or as a recording of a dramatic work.

Musical works

A musical work is a work consisting solely of musical notes, any words or actions intended to be sung, spoken or recorded with the notes are excluded. Therefore, a melody is a musical works with the lyrics being literary.

Artistic works

A wide-ranging definition of artistic works is provided by the CDPA 1988 s.4. Works of architecture are included but focus is usually placed on the remaining artistic works. These fall into two categories:

a) Works protected irrespective of their artistic merit:

    a. Graphic works, i.e. paintings, drawings, diagrams, maps, charts, plans, engravings, etchings, lithographs, woodcuts or similar works

    b. Photographs

    c. Sculptures. The protection of functional objects, such as a cast is problematic. In one notable case in New Zealand Wham-O manufacturing Co v Lincoln Industries Ltd (1985) a wooden model of a Frisbee was held to be a sculpture. The modern UK position is almost certainly more restrictive, as objects will not now be protected as sculptures where they are not made for the purpose of sculpture.

    d. Collages. Collages are artistic or functional visual arrangements produced by affixing two or more items together. Intrinsically ephemeral arrangements (for example the composition of a photograph) are not collages.

b) Artistic works required to be of a certain quality (CDPA 1988 s.4 (1) c i.e. works of artistic craftsmanship. Few works can meet the standard of artistic craftsmanship, as they must be both of artistic quality and the result of craftsmanship. These principles were further developed into a two-part test for artistic craftsmanship in Merlet v Mothercare (1986). First, did the creation of the work involve craftsmanship in the sense that skill and pride was invested in its manufacturer? Second, does the work have aesthetic appeal and did an artist create it?

Sound recordings
A sound recording is a reproducible recording of either:
1) Sounds where there is no underlying copyright work (e.g. birdsong)
2) A recording of the whole or any part of a literary, dramatic or musical work.

The format of recording is of no relevance.

Film
The CDPA 1988 s.5B (1) provides that a film is a reproducible recording of a moving image on any medium. It is the recording itself that is protected, rather than the subject matter that has been recorded, but it should be borne in mind that a film might also be protected as a dramatic work. Film soundtracks are taken to be part of the film itself.

Broadcasts
Copyright subsists in sounds and visual images that are broadcast CDPA 1988 s.6 (1), a broadcast being defined as a transmission by wireless telegraphy of visual images, sounds or other information. The definition of 'broadcast' therefore encompasses radio and television broadcasts and both terrestrial and satellite broadcasting.

Cable programmes
The transmission of an item that forms part of a cable programme will create separate works that are capable of protection as cable

programmes CDPA 1988 s.7. A cable programme service is defined as a service consisting wholly or mainly in sending visual images, sounds or other information via a telecommunications system which may utilise wires or microwave transmission. Items sent via wireless telegraphy are specifically excluded as they are already protected as broadcasts. This means that as well as subscription channels a website on the internet may be a cable programme service.

The typography right

The CDPA 1988 s.8 affords protection to the typography, that is the layout, of published editions of literary, dramatic and musical works. The leading authority on typographical arrangement copyright is Newspaper Licensing Agency Ltd v Marks and Spencer Plc (2001).

Copyright works the ideas/expression dichotomy

There is no copyright in ideas. Copyright subsists in the tangible expression of ideas and not the ideas themselves. In America this is referred to as the ideas/expression dichotomy. This principle can be helpful but should not be taken too literally, as whilst it is clear that mere ideas cannot be protected by copyright the following points should be noted:

1) What might be termed 'highly developed ideas', for example an early draft of a textbook, would be protected by copyright, as are preparatory design material for computer programmes.
2) Copyright cannot be circumvented by selectively altering the expression of a copyright work in the process of reproducing it.

Originality

The CDPA 1988 s.1 requires that literary, dramatic, musical and artistic works be 'original'. The originality requirements only apply to LDMA works, there is no such requirement for secondary copyright works, although it is clear that no copyright will subsist in secondary copyright works that merely reproduce secondary works.

LDMA works must be original in the sense that they originate with the author. One such case that highlights this is University of London Press v University Tutorial Press (1916). This is a minimal qualitative requirement: original works need not be inventive or original and a wide range of works have been held to be original, from coupons for football pools (Ladbrokes v William Hill (1964) to a compilation of broadcasting programmes (Independent Television Publications Ltd and the BBC v Time Out Ltd (1984).

Expending skill and judgement in creating an LDMA work usually suffices to deem the work original. Mere copying cannot confer originality. Alternatively, the mere expenditure of effort or labour (the so-called 'sweat of the brow' test for originality) has sometimes been said to be sufficient to confer originality. But in practice some minimum element of originality is required. For example, in Crump v Smythson (1944) it was held that the generic nature of commonplace diary material left no room for judgement in selection and arrangement therefore the resultant works were not original. Originality has also been held to be more than 'competent draftsmanship' (Interlego v Tyon 1988). Commonly databases and computer programmes were the subject matter of sweat of the brow concerns.

Higher standards of originality: computer programs and databases
As a result of two European Directives, The Directive on the Legal Protection of Databases (Directive 96/9/EC) and the Computer Directive (Directive 91/250/EEC) both computer programmes and databases must be original in the sense that they are the author's own intellectual creation. This is a higher standard or originality than that of 'skills, labour and judgement'.

Some databases may not meet the standard of originality to be afforded copyright protection. In this case the database can be protected by virtue of the *sui generis* database right.

The Database Directive which was incorporated into UK law by Part I11 of the Copyright and Rights in databases regulations 1997 grant a property right in a database whether or not it qualifies for a copyright work. The definition of database includes:

'a collection of independent works, data or other materials arranged in a systematic or methodical way and individually accessible by electronic or other means'.

A database can also be recognised as a literary work and thus afforded copyright protection. For this the database must be original and the contents and arrangements of the database must be a result of the author's own intellectual creation. In any case, all databases are protected by the new database rights irrespective of whether they qualify for copyright protection or not. To qualify for database rights the data must have been assembled through substantial investment in obtaining, verifying and presenting the contents. One case that illustrates this is British Horseracing Board Ltd v William Hill Organisation (2001)).

The duration of the database rights is for 15 years from 1st January of the year following completion of its making, or the first making public of the database within the 15 year period from its making.

Originality and the *de minimis principle*

The question arises, does copyright exist in very short works. The case, Exxon Corporation v Exxon Ind (1982), where the invented word Exxon was denied copyright protection, is often cited to support the proposition that a de minimis principle applies in copyright law, i.e. that some things are too small to be deemed copyright works. However, the authority for this is not so clear.

Fixation and tangibility

As we have seen, copyright does not subsist in literary, dramatic or musical works until they are recorded in writing or otherwise. This pragmatic requirement is known as 'fixation'. Usually, such works will be fixed by the author, but fixation by a third party (with or without the authors permission is also possible. Other copyright works are not subject to the fixation requirement. This is usually unproblematic as films, sound recordings, broadcasts, cable programmes and typography are inherently tangible works.

Ownership of copyright and the employee

The rule is that the first owner of copyright in a work is the person who created the work, i.e. the author. A major exception to this rule is CDPA 1988 s.11 (2). Which provides that where a person creates an LDMA work in the course of employment the employer is the first owner of any copyright in the work subject to any agreement to the contrary. There are special provisions for Crown use, Parliamentary copyright and copyright for certain international organisations (CDPA 1988 s.11 (3).

Authorship, ownership and moral rights

The author is the person who creates the work. Identifying the author is usually a straightforward task. The following is the standard authorship position:

- Literary work. The writer
- Dramatic work. The writer
- Musical work. The composer
- Artistic work. The artist
- Computer generated LDMA works. The person operating the computer.
- Sound recordings. The producer.
- Films. The producer and principal director.

270

- Broadcasts. The broadcaster.
- Cable programmes. The cable program service provider.
- Typography right. The publisher.
- Any work where the identity of the author is unknown. A work of unknown authorship.

Joint authorship

Where more than one person is involved in the creation of a work, careful consideration is needed in determining individual contributions. A person who suggests a subject to a poet is not the author of the poem. Merely supplying ideas is insufficient for joint authorship; an integral role in the expression of ideas is required. Joint authorship arises where the efforts of the two authors is indistinguishable.

For details of changes to copyright Law after BREXIT go to: https://www.gov.uk/government/news/intellectual-property-after-1-january-2021

****

5.4

Design Law

Design

A design may be protected in a number of ways, in particular by the Community Design, (Registered Design and Unregistered Design) the UK Registered Design and the UK Unregistered Design Right. The UK Registered and unregistered design rights have been amended by the introduction of the Intellectual Property Act 2014 which came into force between October 2014 and the end of 2015. This is outlined at the end of this chapter.

Community Design

There are two forms of Community design, one subject to registration (RCD) and the other informal (UCD). The basic requirements are both the same, apart from the date at which novelty and individual character is tested.

A community design has a unitary character and has equal effect throughout the Community. It may only be registered, transferred, surrendered, declared invalid or its use prohibited in relation to the entire community. The main legislation dealing with community design is Article 3 Community Design regulation OJ 2002 L341:

a) 'design' means the appearance of the whole or part of a product resulting from the features of, in particular, the lines, contours, colours, shape, texture and/or materials of the product itself and /or its ornamentation;

b) 'product means any industrial or handicraft item, including *inter alia* parts intended to be assembled into a complex product, packaging, get up, graphic, symbols and typographic typefaces but excluding computer programs:

c) 'complex product' means a product which is composed of multiple components which can be replaced, permitting disassembly and re-assembly of the product.

Article 4 (1) Community Design regulation
A design shall be protected by a community design to the extent that it is new and has individual character.

Novelty and Individual character
A design is new if no identical design (including a design with features which differ only in immaterial details) has been made available to the public. There is a proviso to this and that is a pre-existing design will be disregarded if it could not reasonably have become known in the normal course of business to the circles specialized in the sector concerned operating in the community.

A design has an individual character if the overall impression it produces on an informed user differs from the overall impression produced on such a user by any design which has been made available to the public.

A key case concerning novelty and individual character is that of Green Lane Products Ltd v PMS International Group Ltd (2008). In this case, a challenge to the validity of the claimant's Community design for spiky laundry balls was based on the defendant's similar shaped spiky balls used for massaging the human body.

It was established in this case that the prior art is not limited to the particular product for which the design was registered, as the scope of infringement is not limited to the product for which it was intended to apply the design. For example, the registration of a design intended for motor cars would protect also against its use for toys. The 'informed user' is not the same as the average consumer of trade mark law. The informed user has experience of similar products and will be reasonably discriminatory and able to appreciate sufficient detail to decide whether or not the design under consideration creates a different overall impression. The degree of design freedom is taken into account.

A key case concerning individual character and design freedom is that of Pepsico Inc's design (No ICD000000172) OHIM. he design in question was for a disk having annular rings or corrugations applied to a promotional item for games. There was a challenge to the validity of the design. The design was declared invalid.

The legal principle was that the informed consumer would be familiar with promotional items and would pay more attention to graphical elements rather than minor variations in shape. Furthermore, although there were some constraints to design freedom, these were to do with cost and safety, and, otherwise, there was ample design freedom. Thus, the informed user may focus on certain aspects of a design and design freedom should be looked at in the round and some constraints may be present without significantly reducing the overall design freedom.

Time periods for testing novelty and individual character
The time when a design has been made available to the public differs between the RCD and the UCD (Registered and Unregistered). The RCD relevant date is the date of filing the application, or earlier priority date if there is one. The UCD relevant date is the date the design itself is first made available to the public.

There is a 12-month period of grace for the RCD so, for example the designer may market products relating to that design during that period before filing the application to register. "Under the bonnet' parts which are not seen during normal use of a complex product are not considered to be novel or have individual character.

Exclusions from Community Design
The below are exclusions from community design:

- Features dictated by technical function
- 'Must-fit' features (except in respect of modular systems which are protectable in principle)
- Designs contrary to public policy or morality
- "Must-match' spare parts used to restore the original appearance of a complex product.

Duration

Registered Community Designs – five years from the date of filing. It may then be renewed for further periods of five years up to a maximum of 25 years. Unregistered Community Designs-three years from the date the design was first made available to the public.

For the purpose of the unregistered design in determining the start of the three years, it is made available to the public when it is published, exhibited, used in trade or other wise disclosed in such a way that, in the normal course of the business, these events could have reasonably have become known to the circles specialized in the sector concerned in the community.

Protection and infringement of a community design

The scope of protection of a community design resembles the test for individual character in that it is a question of whether the alleged infringing design, from the perspective of the informed user, does not produce a different overall impression compared with the protected design. Design freedom is taken into consideration.

The main legislation concerning protection of community design is Article 10 Community Design Regulation OJ 2002 L341:

1) The scope of protection conferred by a community design shall include any design which does not produce on the informed user a different overall impression.

2) In assessing the scope of protection, the degree of freedom of the designer in developing his design shall be taken into consideration.

The registered community design gives the rightholder a monopoly right which is infringed by a person using it without the rightholders consent. Use, in particular, includes making, offering, putting on the market, importing, exporting or using a product in which the design is incorporated or applied, or stocking such a product for those purposes.

For the unregistered Community design, it is required that the use in question results from copying the protected design. This also applies during the period of deferred publication where the design is registered but publication has been deferred. An applicant to register a Community design can defer publication by up to 30 months from the filing date, hence delaying the payment of the publication fee.

A key case concerning infringement was that of Procter and Gamble Co v Reckitt Benckiser (UK) Ltd (2008) which was a case on the alleged infringement of a registered Community design applied to a spray container for air fresheners.

It was found in this case that a design did not have to be clearly different, it was sufficient if it differed in a way that the informed user was able to discriminate. An initial decision that there had been an infringement was reversed.

Limitations on the rights to a Community design
The rights to a Community design (registered or unregistered) do not extend to the following acts:

- Acts done privately and for non-commercial purposes.
- Acts done for experimental purposes
- Reproduction for citation or teaching in accordance with fair practices without unduly prejudicing the normal

exploitation of the design, providing the source is mentioned.

- Acts in respect of the repair of ships or aircraft temporarily in the Community.

UK registered design

The UK registered design has been modified as a result of the EU Directive harmonising registered design law throughout the European Community. As a result, the main principles in the EU and UK are virtually identical.

The main legislation dealing with registered designs in the UK is section 24A (2) of the Registered Designs Act 1949 and Regulation 1A (2) Community Design regulations 2005/2339, as amended. In addition, the Intellectual Property Act 2014 has made changes to both UK registered and unregistered designs as outlined below.

UK unregistered design right

The UK unregistered design right was introduced by the Copyright, Designs and Patents Act 1988 in an attempt to overcome the problems of protection of functional designs by means of copyright in drawings showing the designs, as highlighted in *British Leyland Motor Corp v Armstrong patents Co Ltd (1986)*.

The main legislation Section 213(1), (2) and (4) Copyright, Designs and Patents Act 1988, as amended, states:

(1) Design right is a property right which subsists in accordance with this part in an original design.

(2) In this part, 'design' means the design of any aspect of the shape or configuration (whether internal or external) of the whole or part of an article.

(3) A design is not 'original' for the purposes of this part if it is commonplace in the design field in question at the time of its creation.

Exceptions to subsistence of UK unregistered design right
Sections 213 (3) Copyright, Designs and Patents act 1988 states:

(3) Design right does not subsist in -

(a) a method of principle of construction,
(b) features of shape or configuration of an article which -
(i) enable the article to be connected to, or placed in, around or against another article so that either article may perform its function, or
(ii) are dependant upon the appearance of another article of which the article is intended by the designer to form an integral part, or
(c) surface decoration.
The first exception, methods or principles of construction, is unlikely to be relevant in the majority of cases. then other exceptions are often referred to as the 'must fit' or 'must match' exceptions. Surface decoration is also excepted.

A key case in the area is that of Dyson Ltd v Qualtex (UK) Ltd (2006) which concerned various aspects of design right including the scope of the 'must fit' and 'must match' and surface decoration exclusions.

The facts of the case were that the defendant supplied duplicate spare parts (pattern parts) for the claimant's vacuum cleaners. The claimant sued on the basis of the unregistered design rights subsisting in the design of the parts of its vacuum cleaners.

The court found that the 'must fit' exclusion does not mean that the articles have to physically touch. A clearance between them, if it allows one article to perform its function, may be within the exclusion. the exclusion may apply where the two articles are designed sequentially one after the other.

For 'must match' exclusion it is the design dependency which is important. the more room there is for design freedom, the less likely the exception will apply. The reason for the surface decoration exclusion was because it was protected by copyright.

Surface decoration could be applied to a two-dimensional article or three dimensional article or to a flat surface of a three dimensional article. Surface decoration was not limited to something applied to an existing article and it could come into existence with the surface itself. Surface decoration could be three dimensional such as beading applied to furniture. However, a feature having a function, such as ribbing on the handle of a vacuum cleaner, was unlikely to be surface decoration.

The Intellectual Property Act 2014

Stemming from the Hargreaves Review on intellectual property reform, the Act seeks to modernise and simplify certain aspects of intellectual property law including the law relating to designs, in order to promote innovation.

What are the purposes of the changes to design rights?

The purpose of the design right changes are to:

- simplify design law and allow the intellectual property framework to better support innovation
- improve the enforcement of designs and understanding the design rights of others, and
- improve the processes associated with the design framework

What changes are made to design right protection?

Unregistered Designs

- Designer is now the first owner: One fundamental change to existing law is that the act changes the deemed first owner of unregistered designs so that unless otherwise agreed, the designer will be the owner of the designs and not the person who commissioned the designs. Historically the first owner has been the commissioner. This amendment will bring design law into line with UK copyright law

- Trivial design features limited: The definition of Unregistered Design Right has been amended to limit the protection for trivial features of a design
- Clarification of definition of 'design': The act clarifies the definition of design so that to be original a design must not be commonplace in a 'qualifying country' rather than in the 'relevant design field', which caused confusion as to its geographical coverage. Qualifying Country is defined in the Copyright Designs and Patents Act 1988 (CDPA)
- Qualifying Person amended: The act has amended the provisions related to qualifying persons who can claim unregistered design right so that those who are economically active in the EU and other Qualifying Countries (as set out in the CDPA) have protection
- New exceptions to infringement: The act extends the exceptions for infringing unregistered designs, so that acts done privately for no commercial purpose or for teaching will not infringe unregistered design rights. A similar exception applies for acts done for experimental purposes, this is to encourage innovation

Registered Designs

- Designer is now the first owner: The initial ownership position in respect of registered designs is also changed, as for unregistered designs i.e. the designer will be the initial owner unless otherwise agreed, rather than the commissioner.
- New Criminal Offence: The act makes intentional copying of a registered design a criminal offence. This applies to acts which take place in the course of business and the penalties for such an offence are now a fine or prison sentence. Again, this brings the penalties into line with sanctions for trade marks and copyright infringement.

- New exceptions to infringement: The act expands the exception from copyright infringement already available to registered UK designs to registered community designs, i.e. so that an authorised user of a UK or registered community design cannot be sued for infringement of associated copyright.
- Applicant does not need to be the owner of the design: The act removes the requirement for the applicant of a registered design application to be the proprietor of the design.
- New good faith exception to infringement: The act introduces a right of prior use, allowing a third party who has acted in good faith to continue to use a registered design which is subsequently registered by another. The aim of this amendment is to provide an entitlement to limited exploitation in respect of uses already made.
- New powers of enforcement: The act gives Trading Standards officers similar powers of enforcement for design offences as those already available to them in respect of copyright and trade marks.
- Simplified international registration: The act grants power for the Secretary of State to implement the Geneva Act of the Hague Agreement in the UK, this means that international registration procedures will be available for UK registered designs. At present UK designers can only access the Hague registration process via the EU community design registration.
- Harmonisation of financial liability: The act aligns the financial liability provisions for innocent infringement with those provisions under the Community Design Rights legislation.
- Simplified appeal process: The act allows a new route of appeal against Intellectual Property Office (IPO) decisions

via an Appointed Person instead of appealing via the courts, such root already exist for trade mark appeals. This amendment is intended to allow appeals be cheaper and less time consuming.

- New opinions service for ownership, validity and infringement issues: The act provides for a voluntary non-binding opinion service to be introduced by the IPO which is similar to the opinions service which currently exists in respect of patents.
- Clarification: The act clarifies that proceedings for an offence committed against a partnership must be brought against the partnership.
- derived from a continuing programme of research, a report of which is intended for future publication, where disclosure would prejudice the report.

Intellectual Property and Computer Software

Computer software and computer designs have pushed the boundaries of intellectual property law.

All forms of copyright work can exist in digital form and the Copyright, Designs and Patents Act 1988 acknowledges this, for example, by providing that copying includes copying in electronic form and also extends to transient and temporary copies. protection is also given to technological measures to prevent unauthorised acts in relation to computer programmes (in this case called copy-protection) and other forms of works, including databases, have suitable provisions for this. Of particular interest is the protection of computer programs and databases, which may also be protected by a database right.

Computer programs- Computer programs and preparatory design material for computer programs are a form of literary work. Section 3(1) Copyright, Designs and Patents Act 1988 states:

...'literary work' means any work, other than a dramatic or musical work, which is written, spoken or sung, and accordingly includes -

(i) a table or compilation (other than a database);(ii) a computer program;
(iii) preparatory design material for a computer program; and
(iv) a database

For the purposes of copyright a computer programme is original in the sense that it is the author's own intellectual creation. The Act simply requires that a computer program is original, unlike the Directive which uses the above formula.

The basic rules on the restricted acts and infringement apply to computer programs as with other forms of literary work. However, there are some special rules as to what constitutes an adaptation of a compute program and there are some specific permitted acts that apply to computer programs (back-up copies, decompilation, observing, studying and testing and other acts permitted to lawful users). Rules as to ownership are the same as other original works but the nature of the software industry means that many computer programs and other items of software are created by consultants and self-employed persons.

There are no significant issues with respect of duplicate copying of computer programs but non-textual copying can cause problems, such as where an alleged infringer has written a new computer program to emulate the operational and functional aspects of an existing program, sometimes using a completely different computer programming language.

One case that highlights this is Nova Productions Ltd v Mazooma Games Ltd (2007) where the defendant created a computer game which had some similar features to the claimant's game such as the 'power cue'. Both games were based on the game of pool with coloured balls and a green baize table with pockets. The main finding here was that there was no infringement. Although there were similarities, there was no allegation of copying the claimant's program source code. merely emulating an existing program without more does not infringe. the claim was not sufficiently specific to cover copying of the detailed architecture of the claimant's program and merely amounted to a claim to copying general ideas. Jacob LJ said:

'If protection for such general ideas as are relied on here were conferred by the law, copyright would become an instrument of oppression rather than the incentive for creation which it is intended to be. protection would have moved to cover works merely inspired by others, to ideas themselves'.

Databases

It should be noted that although 'computer program' is not defined in the act, there is a definition of 'database' that applies equally to copyright databases and databases protected by the database right even though the two rights are different.

The main definition of a database is that a database is a collection of independent works, data or other materials which are arranged in a systematic or methodical way and are individually accessible by electronic or other means.

Databases can be electronic or other wise. For example, a card index arranged alphabetically would fall within the definition. The contents themselves need not be works of copyright (data or other materials) but if the contents are protected by copyright or other rights, such rights are not prejudiced by the protection of a database as a database.

For the database right to subsist, there must be substantial investment (in terms of human, technical or financial resources) in the obtaining, verification or presentation of the contents of the database. The repeated and systematic extraction and re-utilisation of insubstantial parts of the contents of a database may infringe the database right where, cumulatively. these acts amount to an extraction and/or re-utilisation of a substantial part of the contents of a database measured qualitatively and/ or quantitatively.

Patents and computer software

Certain things are excluded from the meaning of 'invention' for the purposes of patent law. the list of things is not exhaustive, nor is there any deducible common logic between the things excluded. Computer programs, as such, are excluded as are business methods and mental acts. Where there is a 'technical effect' this may overcome the exception but where a computer program only performs other excluded matter, this will not count as a valid technical effect, for example, in the case of a business method implemented by a computer program. The main statute covering this area is Article 52 of the European Patent Convention. This states:

(1) European patents shall be granted for any inventions, in all fields of technology, provided that they are new, involve an inventive step and are susceptible of industrial application.
(2) The following in particular shall not be regarded as inventions within the meaning of paragraph 1:

(a) discoveries, scientific theories and mathematical methods;
(b) aesthetic creations;
(c) schemes, rules and methods for performing mental acts, playing games or doing business, and programs for computers;
(d) presentation of information.

(3) paragraph 2 shall exclude the patentability of the subject matter or activities referred to therein only to the extent to which a European patent application or European patent relates to such subject matter or activities as such.

Design law and computer generated images

Before the harmonisation of registered design law in Europe and the introduction of the Community design, it was almost impossible to register computer graphics as designs in the UK. The definition of 'design' and 'product' under the harmonising directive and the Community Design Regulation changed this. The key statute here is Article 3 (a) and (b) of the Community Design Regulation (Article (1(a) and (b) of the Directive on the legal protection of designs)

(a) 'design' means the appearance of the whole or a part of a product resulting from the features of, in particular, the lines, contours, colours, shape, texture and/or materials of the product itself and/or its ornamentation;
(b) 'product' means any industrial or handicraft item, including *inter alia* parts intended to be assembled into a complex product, packaging, get up, graphic symbols and typographic typefaces, but excluding computer programs.
Although computer programs are expressly excluded, this does not extend to symbols and images generated by computer programs. Also, fonts, being typographical typefaces, are capable of protection.

For details of changes to Design Law after BREXIT go to:
https://www.gov.uk/government/news/intellectual-property-after-1-january-2021

****

Index

Economic loss, 75
Employee inventions, 234
Employee inventor, 234
Employer, 3, 72, 100, 101
Employer's Liability (Defective
   Equipment) Act 1969, 101
Employers Liability, 100
Employers Liability (Compulsory
   Insurance) Act 1969., 100
Employment Appeal Tribunal,
   162
Equal Pay, 164, 165
Equal Pay (amendment)
   Regulations 1983, 164
Equal Pay Act 1970, 164, 165
Errington v Errington (1952), 16
Establishing Authorship, 270
Ex Turpi Causa, 98
Exceptions to infringement, 236
Executory consideration, 33
Exemption clauses, 47
Existing contractual duty to a
   third party, 37
Existing public duty, 35
Express terms of contract, 42
Extent of damage, 91
Extraordinary General Meeting,
   183

Film, 266
Films, 263, 270
Financial Intermediaries,
   Managers and Brokers
   Regulatory Association
   (FIMBRA), 212

Financial loss, 75
Financial Services and Markets
   Act 2000, 211
Fixed and floating charges, 223
Formalities, 27, 71
Frost v Knight (1872), 69

Gaming Act 1845, 59
Gibson v Manchester City
   Council (1979), 9
Glasbrook Brothers v Glamorgan
   County Council (1925), 35
Group structures, 189

Hartley v Ponsonby (1857), 36
Harvey v Facey (1893), 21
Henderson v Arthur (1907), 43
Holiday pay, 142, 143
Hughes v Metropolitan Railways
   Co (1875), 38
Human cloning processes, 231
Hyde v Wrench (1840), 14

Ignorance of the offer, 19
Illegal contract, 61
Illegal mode of performance, 53
Implied terms, 44, 45
Impossible to fulfill contract, 66
Independent contractors, 109,
   113
Infringement, 235, 256
Infringement of a patent, 235
Injunction, 151
Innominate terms, 47
Insider dealing, 221